MoveOn's
50 Ways to Love Your Country

MoveOn's
50 Ways to Love Your Country

HOW TO FIND YOUR POLITICAL VOICE AND BECOME A CATALYST FOR CHANGE

MoveOn

Inner Ocean Publishing, Inc.
Maui, Hawai'i • San Francisco, California

Inner Ocean Publishing, Inc.
P.O. Box 1239
Makawao, Maui, HI 96768-1239

For information on promotions, fund-raising, bulk purchases, premiums, or educational use, please contact: Special Markets, 866.731.2216 or sales@innerocean.com.

Publisher Cataloging-in-Publication Data

MoveOn's 50 ways to love your country : how to find your political voice and become a catalyst for change / by MoveOn – 1st ed. – Makawao, HI : Inner Ocean 2004.

    p. ; cm.

    ISBN: 1-930722-29-X

    1. Political participation—United States. 2. Political science—United States. 3. Nationalism—United States. 4. United States—Politics and government—2001– I. MoveOn

JK1764.M68 2004
323/.042/0973—dc22   0404

With deep respect and appreciation for the intelligence,

creativity, and dedication of the MoveOn members.

You make optimism easy.

Contents

Introduction

Joan Blades and Wes Boyd, Founders, MoveOn

Perhaps the most exciting lesson we've learned at MoveOn is that when people are given a real opportunity to make a difference, they step forward in huge numbers. So, to create this book, we asked MoveOn members to share their stories about how they personally have stepped forward. We were overwhelmed by the response—thousands of stories poured in, in just a few days.

Kate Cox, a 27-year-old New Yorker, described how she regained her balance and perspective after 9/11 by reading diverse sources of information more and watching TV news less. Susan Truax, a working mother in California, managed to make 380 calls (committing herself to 20 at a time) to get out the vote in the California governor's recall election. Michael Fjetland of Texas found a novel way to force his congressional representative, Tom DeLay, to address issues he consistently ignored: Michael ran against DeLay in the Republican primary!

This book is a compilation of contributions—big and small—that MoveOn members have made to the political dialogue. It includes tips and resources, to give everyone the opportunity and knowledge to do more, write more, or speak out more. We have organized the stories into five sections:

- "The Power of Connecting" illustrates how individuals and communities who share ideas and commitment to action can start, sign, and circulate petitions on the Internet, email their elected officials, arrange to meet with their senators, create online media, and research and disseminate candidate information.

- "Every Vote Counts" gives examples of how to further one of the most important actions we take as citizens—by ensuring that our electoral process works, registering voters in innovative ways (including voters often ignored by politicians), and improving voter turnout.

- "The Many Faces of the Media" explores a crucial influence on our political system and public opinion. MoveOn members tell how to become informed media consumers, how to provide several kinds of input to the traditional media, how to counter the conservative spin, and even how to create our own media.

- "Political Action Is Personal" tells the stories of people actively involved in politics, whether supporting bills, starting initiative measures, volunteering in election campaigns, hosting political house parties, donating money, running for office, or developing a fresh campaign strategy.

- "Personal Action Is Political" introduces a broad array of creative steps that people have taken to contribute to the political dialogue, such as expressing political views through art or fashion, engaging in community service, choosing a job in politics, attending a rally or city council meeting, and forming a political salon.

This book is a logical outgrowth of an organization that started quite by accident. In September 1998, six months into the Clinton impeachment mess, we were increasingly frustrated by the paralysis of the government, particularly the failure of our elected leaders to get back to the business of governing. Nobody needed to be educated about the situation anymore. People had well-formed opinions, and the vast majority leaned toward "Get over it! Censure the guy, and get back to the serious business of running this country." But the folks in DC seemed to be living in a parallel universe—one that didn't put the needs of citizens above the advantage to be gained through partisan politics. In response, we sent out a one-sentence petition to fewer than 100 friends and family members: "Congress must immediately censure President Clinton and move on to pressing issues facing the nation."

This was a message that we felt comfortable sending to progressive and conservative friends and family alike. We asked them to sign and tell their friends about it. We all wanted the circus to stop.

Registering www.MoveOn.org, we set up a simple website and quickly learned what it meant for a message to become viral—more than 100,000 people signed our petition in a week! People were grateful. They had been watching a political drama unfold, as they sat by speechless and impotent. At last, they had found a voice and were moved to action.

The massive response put us on the spot. We felt a responsibility for creating this powerful coming together of people. We would certainly deliver the petition, but what next? We had much to learn.

In the following weeks we helped people send emails, make phone calls, and even set up meetings with their members of Congress. And when the House voted to impeach, the MoveOn Political Action Committee (PAC) asked people to support new leadership in Congress. By the time the impeachment fiasco was over, our member list exceeded 500,000 and the MoveOn PAC had millions of dollars pledged for good candidates in the 2000 election.

After that election, we expected to cease operations and leave online activism to established groups. However, our members very much wanted us to continue and made it obvious that our work was not done. So we kept going. Along the way, the MoveOn team has grown to eight incredibly talented and dedicated individuals. Members are familiar with the letters that come from us and Carrie, Peter, Zack, Eli, James, and Noah. Just as we are fortunate to have such passionate members, we are fortunate to have the hardworking and heartfelt partnership of the MoveOn team.

As we grew, we set out to learn what MoveOn members believed were the most pressing issues facing our nation. What were their concerns and hopes? We developed democratic processes for online participation. From email communication, surveys, and our Action Forum, we discovered what members cared most deeply about, and our primary issues for 2001 and 2002 were campaign finance reform and the environment.

Our campaign to avert war in Iraq propelled us onto center stage in 2002. Members had constituent meetings in senate offices in every state of the union, delivering petitions asking for a diplomatic resolution to the situation in Iraq. The Win Without War coalition formed and became a strong voice for peaceful resolution of the conflict; it brought together more than 20 diverse groups—National Council of Churches, Sierra Club, Physicians for Social Responsibility, NAACP, NOW, True Majority, Working Assets, labor groups, and others. MoveOn members made phone calls, wrote letters to the editor, handed out brochures in public places, and marched. When we asked them to support our first ad, a full page in the *New York*

Times headlined "Let the Inspections Work!" members knocked our socks off with their response. We were hoping to raise $35,000; we got $400,000, from more than 10,000 individual contributions.

As of January 2004, we have over 1.8 million active members in the United States. People who haven't had time for politics are reading, talking, asking questions, and engaging. Even better, other groups are connecting online: the AFL-CIO presently has 1.2 million online activists; Planned Parenthood has more than 400,000; and the Natural Resources Defense Council has more than 600,000. As people connect with the political dialogue on issues they care about, it's only a matter of time before our politicians will better reflect our values.

We set high standards for things we love. Because we love our country—our freedoms, our diversity, and our traditions—we strive to help our country be its best. We feel blessed to live in a country where we have the freedom to speak out, the right to assemble, and the tradition of political action by ordinary citizens.

After hearing the more than 2,500 stories of personal action and paring the book down to 50 essays (boy, was this difficult!), we are in awe of our contributors and trust that their stories will dispel any foolish cynicism about public apathy. Whenever we feel overwhelmed, we read these narratives, and we are inspired.

Engagement in the political dialogue—large or small—breathes life into us all. Thank you for all you do.

I: The Power of Connecting

Introduction

Peter Schurman, Executive Director, MoveOn

W e live in the third century of the world's most important political experiment: the founding of an American democracy "of, by, and for the people." The founders were well aware of the forces aligned against democracy— greed, avarice, ambition—so they designed an elaborate system of checks and balances to dampen these dark impulses and to unleash our instincts to work together and build a better future for our children.

Today, there are reasons for deep concern. Democracy is threatened by two forces that may swamp the dream of government by the people: the power of corporate money and the power of the media. But just as technology has created the modern media and the modern multinational corporation, technology has also given individuals an amazing new ability to connect to each other and take action together. This newfound ability to connect is transforming politics.

Connecting is the key. It's the only way we can preserve democracy.

The Internet presents the best opportunity we've had in decades to make connecting easier, quicker, and cheaper. And the millions of people connecting through organizations like True Majority, Common Cause, People for the American Way, Sierra Club, AFL-CIO, Natural Resources Defense Council, Working Assets, and MoveOn are proving that it works. Together, organizations big and small are winning more victories, stopping parts of the right-wing agenda in its tracks, and sometimes even passing visionary legislation like a new California law that can help the whole country curtail greenhouse gas emissions.

Connecting online offers certain basic, compelling advantages. The contributors in this section describe how to use them, so I'll simply list them here. Online contact is:

- Inexpensive: For example, when you set up an online petition, the cost for each new person is almost zero.

- Effective: Thousands of voices can come together quickly online and count heavily with legislators, who often hear nothing from constituents but a lot from paid lobbyists.

- Motivating: Once you take the first step of forming connections online, you can build relationships online and off and take increasingly powerful actions.

We've got to remember to reach outside our circles of comfort. Especially on the Internet, it's easy to isolate ourselves in like-minded communities and to pay attention to only news sources that confirm our beliefs. In a polarized society like ours today, it can be difficult to remember that we must engage in respectful dialogue and build on our shared values with those who disagree with us on some issues.

I have traveled across the country a couple of times, and, wherever I've gone, I've met people who shared certain basic values: civility, optimism, a commitment to do the right thing. I've found these values just as often in states considered "conservative," like Indiana and Idaho, as in "progressive" states, like Massachusetts and California—or even more often.

America is held together by an overwhelming majority of people who share a basic belief in leaving a better world for future generations and who are willing to fight for it if given an opportunity.

Connecting online can provide that opportunity. Like the contributors in this section, we can connect with others and together turn our country around.

Create an Effective Online Petition

Dorothy Keeler, 51, Anchorage, Alaska

The wolves of Denali National Park were in danger, and we had to spread the word fast.

As wildlife photographers, my husband and I have worked with the Toklat wolves in Denali since 1990. The Toklat and Sanctuary wolves had been seen and enjoyed by tens of thousands of visitors each year inside the park. They were remarkably accepting of humans at close distances, making them unique among wild wolves. However, during the winter, both packs would leave the safety of the park on hunting forays, where they were routinely trapped and killed. Near the park entrance, the entire Sanctuary pack was killed by trappers. The Toklat family dropped from a high of 18 members in the early 1990s to just 2 in 1998. Luckily, the 2 were an alpha male and alpha female, which are the leaders of the pack, who mated and had pups the next year. When the Sanctuary pack was killed off, a nearby group, the Margaret pack, moved into their territory.

In 2001, our friends at the Alaska Wildlife Alliance submitted a proposal to the Alaska Board of Game (the wildlife-policy decision maker) to create a no-kill "buffer zone" adjacent to the park, covering the areas the remaining packs were known to frequent. The Board of Game would decide the fate of the buffer zone at an upcoming meeting, and the hunting lobby was already using heavy-handed political pressure. Though more than 80 percent of Alaskans were wildlife viewers, the Board of Game was composed entirely of hunters and trappers, who were dead set against additional hunting restrictions.

Facing such odds, we had to show massive support for protecting the packs. With the Board of Game meeting just a week away, I created a simple website that included a summary of the issue and photos showing why the wolves deserved special protection. I then established a petition on www.thepetitionsite.com, asking signers to answer questions in order to personalize the petition.

With only a week's time, I had to jump-start the word-of-mouth process. First I sent the e-card to everyone in my address book. Then I sent it to the leaders of every environmental group I could find in Alaska. Next I wrote a short press release. Finally I composed a letter to the editor that summarized the issue and included the URL of the website, and I sent that to every newspaper in Alaska.

Almost 1,000 people signed our petition, from every state in the union and more than 36 countries. I called the local newsrooms to say I'd be wheeling boxes of signed petitions into the Board of Game meeting on a hand truck. We made the six o'clock news, and the petition helped convince the Board of Game to create the buffer zone. At the moment, the wolves are protected by the buffer zone, thanks in part to all those wonderful people who signed the petition. However, there are still pressures against wolves and the environment in Alaska, and we're standing by.

MoveOn Tips

- Make a targeted website the center of your campaign. Make certain everything on the site relates to the action you want visitors to take.

- Create a petition at www.thepetitionsite.com.

- Spread your message through emails and electronic post-cards, which are similar to the electronic birthday cards many people send online. Dorothy Keeler used http://mypost-cards.com, a site that offers several postcard web hosting services, including a free service.

- Write a letter to the editor that gives a reference to your web-site. This improves the odds that locals will sign the petition, and it saves the cost of buying an expensive ad.

Dorothy Keeler is a professional wildlife photographer/activist who lives with her husband, Leo. The Keelers have appeared on *CBS News* in regard to their conservation efforts, and they're now moving their entire business to www.akwildlife.com so they'll have more time for activism.

Spread the Word about Online Petitions

Bich Ngoc Cao, 21, Los Angeles, California

In September 2001, California Assembly Bill (AB) 25, a comprehensive domestic partners bill, won passage in the legislature through a statewide grassroots campaign using foot soldiers and mouse clicks. I had the pleasure of helping the campaign gain momentum, and, when I received the news that it had passed, I thought jubilantly, "Something great just happened, and I got to be a part of it!"

Just a year before, I'd been furious at the success of the Knight initiative, which legally defined marriage as a union between a man and a woman. Since gay marriage was not a legal option before the initiative, I felt the additional legislation served only to divide Californians.

Equal rights proponents fought back, and I joined the campaign. On the ground, civil rights organizations and lesbian/gay/bisexual/transgender (LGBT) community groups organized people to attend festivals, concerts, farmers' markets, and other public gatherings to garner voter signatures on a petition urging the legislature and Governor Gray Davis to pass AB 25. On the Internet, volunteers like me gathered signatures from their friends by email. I appealed to my friends' sense of equality, telling them about the basic—not special—rights that the bill would confer on domestic partners, such as the right to make medical decisions on behalf of an incapacitated partner.

It was the first time I had reached out to friends and family members on a hugely controversial issue, so instead of mass emailing everyone I knew, I looked into my address book and wrote personalized emails asking people to sign the petition.

To my surprise, I received about 60 signatures within a few days, mostly from friends whom I hadn't envisioned as gay rights supporters. My own brother, who'd always mocked my passion for politics, even forwarded my email to his friends. I just couldn't believe the response.

Of course, I got some flak, too. The funniest response was, "You're not gay. Why do you care?" I had to repeatedly tell people that I didn't need to be gay to care about LGBT rights, since AB 25 dealt with basic rights that all people should have.

Overall, people understood and empathized with our message of equality. When Governor Gray Davis signed the bill into law in October 2001, ACLU spokesperson Christopher Calhoun reported, "For the first time in California's history, there were more letters, phone calls, emails, and faxes in support of an LGBT civil rights bill than in opposition." Of course, the far right hadn't stopped opposing gay rights—our campaign had simply mobilized the people who care about civil rights.

I was enthralled that I had helped pass a bill by using the Internet. It had been easy and quick, even though I'd written emails one by one. Since then, I've emailed my friends dozens of times about various political issues, but I might not be so bold if I hadn't tried it that first time and succeeded so overwhelmingly.

MoveOn Tips

- To be most effective, write to each person individually, explaining why this issue is important to you and letting your friends and family know how they can help.

- If you can't write individual letters, write your email to appeal to a wide audience. Respect the views of people who disagree; being confrontational won't persuade, it'll only offend.

- Include primary sources and resources in your email, so your friends and family know where to find more information.

- Don't email people too often, lest they become annoyed at you.

Bich Ngoc Cao is a print journalism and political science student at the University of Southern California in Los Angeles. She is a self-described Internet geek.

Sign a Petition

David Lynch, 45, Asheville, North Carolina

Until a year ago, I'd never been very active politically, even though I'd spent most of my life unhappy with the status quo. I voted religiously and wrote the occasional letter to the editor, and I never imagined I'd ever be more involved in political affairs.

That all changed when I signed MoveOn's antiwar petition to avert war in Iraq. Shortly thereafter, MoveOn contacted me via email and asked me to lead a delegation to present the petition's state signatures to Senator John Edwards's field office in North Carolina. The whole process of arranging the meeting and organizing attendees was new to me, but I stumbled through, and in the end brought more than 35 concerned citizens and the thick MoveOn petition of more than 3,400 North Carolina signatures to Senator Edwards's desk. We were covered by the local newspaper, too.

I walked out of his office feeling empowered. I had tapped into personal talents and capabilities I didn't know I had. The end of that meeting was a beginning for me. That day I had lunch with other local activists— and I've worked with many of them frequently ever since. I was invited to the Western North Carolina Peace Coalition meetings. The next thing I knew, I was involved.

I attended two Washington, DC, antiwar protests, helped organize peace rallies in my hometown, and joined with another MoveOn delegation to protest the war at the local office of our congressional representative. Local newspaper, TV, and radio media began seeking me out for interviews. I kept writing editorials, many of which were published in our local paper; and one piece I wrote made it onto the website www.alternet.org. I also used my professional graphic design skills to create posters, flyers, banners, and handouts that helped bring unprecedented numbers of people to our peace rallies.

I feel like I'm giving back to my community and my country in ways I didn't know I could. Though I expected no personal return for my efforts, this glorious work has brought me closer to the people around me and given me a sense of connection I've never before experienced. I may not have changed the world just yet, but I've made the important first step: I changed myself.

MoveOn Tips

- Sign online petitions on the websites of reputable organizations. You can do this by going to the websites of the organizations you most want to support. Many, like MoveOn, allow you to subscribe to email newsletters that alert you to important current events and petitions responding to those events. They also generally provide you with the contact numbers of your senators and representatives and tips for points to make when you contact elected officials.

- Opt for petitions circulated by email that provide a link you can click to go to a specific site. Once there, you can read the petition and add your name at that centralized location. We've all received forwarded email petitions that ask us to type in our name at the bottom of the email itself and forward it to our friends. Every 50th or 100th person is supposed to return the email to a designated email address where the petitions are supposedly compiled. This method was developed in the early days of Internet technology, and it isn't the best way to petition for or against an issue. Signatures often don't make it into the intended hands, and the emails tend to circulate long after the bill or initiative has been decided.

David Lynch is a graphic designer, activist, and old-time fiddle player living in the mountains of western North Carolina.

Share Informed Political Recommendations
Michael Rosenthal, 48, Fairfax, California

S ome 25 years ago I got tired of the political action committees (PACs) to which I had been contributing. I felt that they weren't putting my donations to the best use. They supported many candidates who were virtually guaranteed to win the election. They also attempted to maintain a bipartisan veneer by endorsing some Republicans. I wanted my money used where it would do the most good: for progressive Democrats involved in close races.

In 1982, I did some research and picked two Senate races that I felt met my guidelines. I made modest contributions directly to the Democratic candidates in those contests. Lo and behold, one of my candidates won in an upset! (The candidate, Jeff Bingaman from New Mexico, is still in the Senate today. His voting record is tremendously better than that of the right-wing Republican he defeated.) Now, I'm not claiming that my meager financial contribution made the difference, but this was more like it.

Buoyed by this success, I decided to expand my research and provide recommendations to like-minded friends who might want to support such candidates, too. I published the first "Progressive Election Alert" in 1980, and I've put out a new one every election cycle since. It highlights several key Senate races across the country in an easily digested form, and it's helped raise money for more than 100 candidates so far.

But the contributions generated are only a small part of the story. As a result of the "Progressive Election Alert," people started asking me for voting recommendations. In California, our ballot sometimes contains so many candidates and initiatives that the official Voters' Guide comes in two volumes! Figuring out how to vote can be overwhelming, even for those of us who consider ourselves well-informed. So I began researching election issues, printing my own ballot recommendations, and distributing them to family, friends, and acquaintances.

The response has been tremendous. Friends have been incredibly grateful. "I don't know what I'd do without your picks!" is a typical comment. I know for a fact that many people take my list to the polls with them; some even distribute it to their friends.

I still put out the "Progressive Election Alert" every two years, though I'm convinced its offshoot, "Mike's Picks," has a far greater impact. The easier we make it for people to access the information they need to make intelligent choices, the better the turnout will be on Election Day, and the better the election will turn out.

MoveOn Tips

- To have the most impact, give your information to people who know you.

- Make the information as concise and readable as possible.

- Develop a network of politically active people whom you respect that you can draw upon for information and opinions.

- Get your information out as early as possible. Many people use absentee ballots, and they often fill them out well before Election Day.

- Share your passion and information on the issues by educating people instead of "telling" them how to vote. Provide them with resources so they can research further if they choose.

- If you can, minimize your work, make it more fun, and multiply your efforts by gathering a few friends to debate and jointly figure out ballot recommendations. Then you can use all of your group's contacts to spread your recommendations as widely as possible.

Michael Rosenthal is a local television producer/writer in the San Francisco Bay Area. He lives in a former train station with his wife and a cat. His "Progressive Election Alert," "Mike's Picks," and more can be found on his website, www.mikespac.org.

Speak Out Online

Michael Tulipan, 33; James Linkin, 52, New York, New York

When James and I started developing OutrageRadio, our online liberal talk radio program, we knew we'd be facing pretty stiff challenges. *Liberals don't listen to commercial radio. The Internet is dead. This president is unbeatable.* We'd heard it all. It seemed the odds were stacked against anyone who might criticize or disagree with the president, but we were both looking for a way to stand up, especially to the media conglomerates.

Then, independently of each other, we both found MoveOn. I heard of the antiwar campaign and was very impressed by the response, especially the amount of money raised on the Internet. James was intrigued by the effectiveness and the sheer elegance of use of the Internet to bring intelligent people of conscience together.

One day, in the middle of early planning for OutrageRadio, we each received a notice that Al Gore was going to speak to MoveOn members at New York University on August 7, 2003. I RSVP'd immediately and added James as my guest. Coincidentally, James had done the same, and we were double-booked! Surprisingly, we had never talked about being MoveOn members until that day. Needless to say, we went to the speech and were heartened to see that dissent was not dead in America.

From that point, inspired by MoveOn's grassroots success and with new faith in the Internet's power, we redoubled our efforts to launch www.OutrageRadio.com. For most of the year, we developed the program at a sound studio in New York City. Finally, in October 2003, we launched a preview website with an audio trailer. The response to the site was immediate as we received press, coverage in the blogosphere, and emails wishing us well from across the country. The next month, we launched an upgraded version of the site complete with the first program, "Homeland Insecurity." In our first two months, www.OutrageRadio.com received more than 80,000 hits.

As we promote ourselves and build our audience, we view MoveOn's success as a recipe that we, and really anyone, can follow. The first thing is to develop a clear message, and then publicize it and manage it as it builds through public awareness. Use every tool you can to get the message out—that's our motto.

MoveOn Tips

Although Michael and James had access to a professional sound studio, starting an online radio program can be done easily and inexpensively at home. But first you need to have a clearly defined goal—is this a hobby or the start of a new career in radio? That decision dictates how much time and money you put into the project.

- To start a radio program at home, be sure to have a good PC or Mac (ideally less than a year old) with a microphone and a sound recording program.

- Design a professional website, even if it costs you some money. Many websites are overlooked because of poor design.

- Use a reliable Internet service provider to host the site. Ask your website developer or any techie for a recommendation. Michael and James use Jumpline, and they've found it works well.

- Decide which formats you will stream, and make sure your ISP supports them. Windows, Real, and Quicktime all have basic streaming software with simple interfaces that you can download free. Record to MP3, and import the file into the appropriate software. Then upload the files to your site.

- Promote. Promote. Promote. Tell your friends, invite guests, write a blog. Just get the name and URL out there.

Michael Tulipan and *James Linkin* are cofounders of OutrageRadio, Liberals with Attitude. They are media veterans and victims of the dot-com crash who decided to use their know-how to fight back against the right-wing domination of talk radio.

Email the President (and Other Politicians)

Cynthia B. Sosnowski, 51, Stone Harbor, New Jersey

In recent times, it seems as if all disagreement with the current administration has been labeled "unpatriotic," "un-American," or "soft on terror." I was increasingly frustrated with my own sense of disempowerment, so I decided to join the vocal dissenters and do my part in letting the president know on a daily basis that dissenting voices are many and varied.

I changed my home page to www.news.google.com, which provides U.S. and international news reports side by side, so that I could scan the world headlines every morning. Now, each day when I first go onto the Internet, I browse the headlines and choose one that I think reflects logical dissent from or questioning of the administration's position. I go to the link and read the entire piece. If it is well written and supported, I email it to George W. Bush at president@whitehouse.gov. I also email it to Dick Cheney at vice.president@whitehouse.gov.

Since the White House has instituted a new and unimproved process for email correspondence, the system sends back an auto-reply thanking me for my letter and suggesting that I also go to the White House website and send a comment that way. I use the link provided and dash off a suitable postscript to the original message. The whole process takes only a few minutes, and Bush gets two messages from me every day. Maybe no one reads these emails carefully, but I'm betting they're at least counted, and perhaps they're scanned for dissenting or assenting opinion language.

This has become a habit as ingrained as my morning coffee, and my husband's standing joke is that I must have a relationship with someone in the White House, because a person named "Auto Responder" writes to me every morning.

MoveOn Tips

- Mail a letter to the White House:
  The White House
  1600 Pennsylvania Avenue, NW
  Washington, DC 20500

- Call or fax the White House:
  Comments: 202-456-1111
  Switchboard: 202-456-1414
  Fax: 202-456-2461
  TTY/TDD Comments: 202-456-6213
  Visitors' Office: 202-456-2121

- Email the White House:
  President George W. Bush: president@whitehouse.gov
  Vice President Richard Cheney:
  vice.president@whitehouse.gov

- Write your representative at www.house.gov/writerep/.
  Simply type in your state and zip code and this service will
  direct you to your representative through an email form.

- Get a list of representatives' and committees' websites at
  www.house.gov/.

- Find complete House member information including
  addresses and phone numbers at clerk.house.gov/.

- Find information for contacting your senators, including
  addresses, phone numbers, and email addresses or forms at
  www.senate.gov/general/contact_information/senators_
  cfm.cfm.

- Bookmark www.firstgov.gov/Contact.shtml, which provides
  links for contacting all federal agencies.

Cynthia B. Sosnowski is assistant to the dean of social and behavioral sci-
ences at Richard Stockton College of New Jersey.

Meet with Your Representatives

Naomi Warren, 22, Greenwood, Indiana

I attended a liberal arts college on the East Coast with a multicultural student body. When I returned to Indiana after graduation, I struggled with the culture shock of moving from a diverse and tolerant region of the country to one that seemed to lack both qualities. As I tried desperately to fill the emptiness of being away from everything I had known for four years, I happened upon MoveOn. After reading the site, I suddenly felt a renewed purpose; here was an online environment in which I could again question politics and remember the importance of my place, as an American citizen, in the political spectrum.

I began to take action: I contacted my senators and representatives about my concerns regarding the environment and health care; I wrote letters to the editor in an attempt to explain that one could be both antiwar and pro-soldier; and I began conversing with co-workers and strangers about their political views. I would alternate between feeling encouraged and feeling defeated, depending on whether our cumulative actions seemed to be making a difference. Through MoveOn, I connected with Working Assets, which contacted me about meeting with my senators. I signed up to do that, simply because I had participated in every other action/event that MoveOn had promoted. I never expected that this simple meeting would so elucidate my understanding of democracy.

At first, I gave little thought to the meeting I was to attend with Indiana's Republican Senator Richard Lugar. Emails among those of us who were to meet with him fluttered around for days and weeks prior, until finally the day arrived. I woke up feeling nervous. I went to work thinking that I should back out. I felt silly attending. What could I, a 22-year-old with little political experience, have to add? I almost felt guilty, because I knew that the slots were limited, and I felt extremely underqualified to be going (forgetting that all constituents are created equal). As I walked to Senator Lugar's office, though, I tried to focus my attention and memorize the statistics I had researched the days before.

When I arrived, I was greeted by Charlie, the man who had volunteered to organize our meeting with Senator Lugar. He was as friendly as he had seemed in email, and one by one the rest of the participants arrived. By the time we sat down to meet with Lugar's press secretary and deputy director (the senator, unfortunately, was out of the country at the time of our visit), I had already come to feel a sense of camaraderie with the rest of the group. These people had almost immediately become my friends and family, simply as other Americans—Indiana "Hoosier" Americans—putting the ideals of democracy into action.

The meeting was amazing. We took turns during the hour to introduce ourselves, tell personal stories, and give voice to our shared concerns. We were Democrats. We were Republicans. We were men. We were women. We were single, married, old, young, antiwar activists, and war veterans. And yet, the 13 of us shared one vision and one simple expectation—that Lugar's representatives would let the senator know that his constituents cared about the United States initiating a preemptive war with Iraq and that we expected him to act with integrity on an issue important to all of us.

I left the meeting feeling more empowered than I had in many months, if not years. It seemed like such a simple act—after all, we had only contacted one of our legislators. And yet, those contacts prove incredibly powerful. Indeed, they make a great difference.

MoveOn Tips

- Sign online petitions that reflect your beliefs. Doing so can lead to a sense of community and connection, and it allows you to play a more active role in the democratic process.
- Find an online community that you can join to help you stay connected and informed.

Naomi Warren works for a nonprofit organization in Indianapolis, Indiana, and lives in a small town south of the city.

II: Every Vote Counts

Introduction

Al Gore, Former Vice President

W oody Allen has famously said that 90 percent of success is showing up. That's true of democracy too. I'd argue that the other 10 is making sure you're registered beforehand.

It's easy to be cynical about politics and to believe that one vote barely matters. But consider these facts: John F. Kennedy's 1960 victory over Richard Nixon—a victory that ultimately led to sweeping changes in civil rights laws, the first great wave of space exploration, and the creation of Medicare—was decided by just 100,000 votes nationwide. In 1994, the year Republicans won both houses of Congress, the redistribution of about 10,000 votes nationally would have kept Congress in Democratic hands. One of my former House colleagues, Connecticut Democrat Sam Gejdenson, won reelection by twenty-one votes that year. ("All you need is one," he remarked; "the rest are for your ego.")

The democratic political process isn't perfect. Winston Churchill once said it's the worst system for governance "except for every other system that has ever been tried." Often, you may find no candidate who completely reflects your views. But as voter participation has declined—from nearly two-thirds of eligible voters in 1960 to less than half in many national elections today—strong and decidedly undemocratic forces have stepped in to fill the void.

In a democracy, the future isn't something that just happens; it's something we shape for ourselves, together. Special-interest lobbyists get the government they pay for only when we stay home from the polls—only when we abdicate the electoral power that is mightier than any soft-money check, more decisive than any million-dollar ad blitz or corporate misinformation campaign.

Ironically, it is sometimes the most idealistic citizens who are the most reluctant to participate in our electoral processes—to try to improve our decidedly imperfect world. But I believe in the words of Mahatma Gandhi: "We must become the change we wish to see in the world." And that change doesn't necessarily come in a single election. Dramatic social changes such as desegregation, civil rights, Medicare and Medicaid, national service corps, and economic opportunity programs were ideas that built support over time—losing at the ballot box initially, but ultimately triumphing and transforming the country.

In just a handful of months, MoveOn has begun to show the strength and breadth of the grass roots in this country; it has shown how many people are eager to make their mark on our political system, in ways large and small. This book is a powerful demonstration of the myriad opportunities to do so.

'Voting is how we come together, as Americans and as believers in self-rule. There is no greater or more profound right of citizenship. Take it from this veteran of a close and controversial election: The process matters. Sometimes you win, sometimes you lose. And then there's that little-known third category. But democracy wins when all of us get in gear and participate with enthusiasm and passion and heartfelt commitment. Now is the time. You are the answer.

Vote, No Matter What

Murray Hirsh, 79, Pembroke Pines, Florida

In 1996, I was in charge of the day-to-day operations of the Clinton/Gore reelection campaign headquarters in Pembroke Pines, Florida. On a Saturday morning two weeks before the election, I opened the office at about 8:15. Volunteers were scheduled to arrive at 9:00.

The phone immediately rang. The person on the other end told me she was a hospice nurse. She was in the home of a man who had only days to live but who'd received his absentee ballot. He knew who he wanted to vote for, but he had questions about some of the complicated wording of the referenda.

He would not live long enough to know who won the presidency or what initiatives had passed, but he was concerned, on his deathbed, to be sure he voted intelligently for the betterment of his fellow citizens.

Here was a man whom I never met, whose name I did not know, and I don't know when he died, but he taught me something I will never forget: the importance of one man's vote.

MoveOn Tips

- Register to vote at www.workingforchange.com/vote/.

- Go to www.fec.gov/votregis/vr.htm to print out copies of the National Voter Registration form, which is good in most states (see the site for details).

- You may request an absentee ballot by contacting your local county or city election official. Also, www.fvap.gov/links/state links.html will take you to the official sites of the Secretaries of State and/or Directors of Elections in your community.

Murray Hirsh works 25 hours a week as a courier and at a desk in a city office processing payments for water, sewer, and trash pickup.

Mobilize Underrepresented Voters

Lillie Coney, 43, Burtonsville, Maryland

In Beaumont, Texas, 1978 was a political year like any other except for one little-noted difference—a small office downtown, staffed by three African-American activists. There weren't many African-American businesses in the city at the time, and even fewer downtown. The new office and its staff trio were designated a Get Out the Vote (GOTV) project, funded by a local Democratic power base. They would focus their efforts on the underrepresented, politically nascent African-American community.

Leading this GOTV effort was Dennis Graham, the first black professional political organizer I had ever met. Under his leadership, we registered voters from minority groups, with the hope that those in power would take notice and that new political activists would emerge from the masses of the newly registered.

We began by bringing voter registration opportunities to people at churches, parks, public events, and shopping centers. We also went to local, state, and federal offices that provided services to nontraditional voters. Very productive locations included the local public assistance office serving low-income mothers under the Women, Infants, and Children Nutrition program, the county and city public health offices, unemployment offices, senior citizen service centers, and locations where water and other public utility bills were paid. I would add to this list bingo night. Our method dramatically increased the number of registered voters from one or two per household to as many as six. Families were commonly seen going to the polls together, which encouraged neighborhoods to vote at record numbers. Voter participation in the African-American community living in Jefferson County and Texas City increased dramatically from averages between 26 and 47 percent to more than 50 percent during that year's primary election and nearly 80 percent for the November election.

The local political projections about election outcomes turned out to be inaccurate, since they were based on past voter participation (when there was low black voter turnout). The unanticipated increase in black voter participation increased margins of victory, and the dynamics of political influence drastically shifted. The once-ignored black vote became a symbol of raw political power, with enough influence to determine the outcome of critical local, state, and federal primary and general elections.

Despite—or perhaps because of—our rousing success, fiscal support of future GOTV projects seemed to dry up. Nonetheless, the events of 1978 led to a decade of profound change in local politics—a shift in the balance of power. For the first time in the city's history, the school board became a body of members from minority communities. The city council gained substantial minority representation. The first African-American member of the Jefferson County Commissioners Court was elected. During this same time, I ran for my first and only elected office and won: precinct captain for Jefferson County Precinct 18.

The current state of politics in the United States only energizes me because of my personal experience with the one-person-one-vote rule that we cherish in this nation. The idea that one person cannot make a difference is disproved every day in small and great ways by average people fully expressing their God-given free will. We, the people, are the government, and it is time for us to remind those we can hire and fire each Election Day of this fact. I love being an American, and to me that means thinking and acting independently based on my principles and beliefs.

MoveOn Tips

- Contact the county office that manages elections (usually part of the county government or the state secretary of state's office) to learn the rules for registering voters in your county. Be sure to ask the following questions: Can registered voters be deputized to register people living in the county or anywhere in the state? Can family members register each other —for example, can spouses register each other and their children, and can children register their siblings and their parents?

- Write a brief description of your plan to register voters and send it to organizations with a history of funding voter registration projects (such as labor unions, the NAACP, local Democratic organizations, the National Political Party, and individual campaigns). Tell them how many new voters you expect to register, in which county you'll be working, and your deadline for completion.

- Recruit family and friends to help in the registration drive. Consider asking for help from sororities, fraternities, churches, local clubs, professional groups, and the like.

- When your drive is over, bring the voter registration cards to the campaign office or compile a list of all newly registered voters. On the list include each new voter's name, address, phone number, and if possible email address. Some campaigns pay a bounty for newly registered voters, but to collect the reward you need to verify that a voter is not already registered. In many jurisdictions the voter registration lists are public information and provide the name, address, and registration ID of all registered voters. Usually no fee is charged to look at the list, but a small reproduction fee may be charged if you want a copy of the list.

Lillie Coney worked for two African-American women members of Congress prior to becoming the public policy coordinator for the Association for Computing Machinery. She is passionate about our democracy and believes in fighting to preserve it for future generations.

Register Voters in Unlikely Places

Saskia Traill, 30, San Francisco, California

I first got involved in local politics in San Francisco in 1999. Just three and a half weeks before the mayoral election that year, a few inspired individuals organized a write-in campaign for a candidate who represented all the progressive values that none of the other candidates espoused.

With just $25,000 to purchase Write In Tom Ammiano for Mayor pens, buttons, window signs, and door hangers teaching people how to write in a candidate, Ammiano made it to a runoff election, beating candidates who'd spent millions of dollars and had battalions of paid staff. Around town, people who had never cared about politics were getting excited. Young people who had just moved to the city were showing up at the campaign headquarters to help. Those who no longer cared about the electoral process were starting to feel like they had a voice again.

My friends capitalized on this new excitement by organizing a voter registration drive, which I took part in. Lots of the city's newcomers, young people, and politically disenchanted residents were not registered to vote. This is true everywhere, and, for progressive politics, getting these folks registered is the first step to winning. We didn't go to the usual campaign hot spots such as supermarkets and street fairs. Instead, we went where we knew a lot of these people were likely to be. We hit the bars.

Starting around 9:00 P.M., six of us formed pairs, put on signs saying "Register to Vote Here," and grabbed clipboards. We went table to table and barstool to barstool registering people and talking about the campaign. I met new people and ran into old friends. I explained why voting was important, why I supported my candidate, what the runoff was all about, and how people could get more information about the election and their vote.

At the end of every night, we stopped and had a beer at the last bar on the route, laughing about funny conversations and sharing our favorite stories of the night. I registered someone who asked if there was an Anarchist party he could join. Someone else registered a 68-year-old man who had never voted in his life. And somebody else made her best attempt to pull out her high school Spanish and apparently asked a woman if she was registered to bounce.

Our candidate lost the runoff, but the following year there was a progressive sweep of the Board of Supervisors that by all accounts originated with the excitement from the 1999 write-in campaign. I worked on one supervisor's campaign and met one of those inspired individuals who started the write-in. I married him a few years later.

Through the process of registering voters, I learned to talk to friends and strangers about why I care about politics and why I hope they will too, all the while having fun. To me this is what grassroots politics is all about. And it works.

MoveOn Tips

- Voter registration forms include two languages. Make sure you get the most appropriate ones for the area you're canvassing.

- Bring pens, something to write on, and a small flashlight if it'll be dark.

- Wear a Register to Vote Here sign or button to let people know what you're doing and save your voice in noisy places.

- Familiarize yourself with the registration form and your candidate's history and views or the issue you're campaigning about, but don't worry if you don't know everything. Offer people a website address where they can get more information.

- Explain why you personally support the issue or candidate.

- Have fun. If someone disagrees with you, just say thanks and move on. Reconnect with the other volunteers, and laugh about it. Show people you're enjoying yourself, and they'll want to volunteer too.

Saskia Traill is a researcher and writer at a nonprofit public policy and law organization.

Organize an Issue–Specific Voter Registration Drive

Terrill Legueri, 20, Denver, Colorado

I am passionate about two issues: citizen involvement in local and national politics, and the environment. However, my ranting and raving at election time about "civic duty" and "protecting the earth from corporate polluters" often seemed to fall on deaf ears. I wanted people to get involved and care, but shouting at them didn't seem to be working.

When I returned to college in the fall of my second year, my friend Claire suggested that we run a voter registration drive that focused on the environment for the upcoming election. During the summer she had worked with an organization that concentrated on getting people to vote on environmental issues, and she thought we could mount a campaign on our campus. I was definitely interested.

She suggested that we spend more time on providing information and less time on heckling, and I agreed that coming from a place of anger isn't as effective as rational thinking, facts, and sound logic. In fact, I was inspired. I spent the next two weeks researching all the candidates running in the election. This time, instead of focusing on only the candidates that I felt were making progress in safeguarding the environment, we used a bipartisan approach: we created a spreadsheet displaying the candidates, their party affiliation, and where they stood on key environmental issues based on their voting history. We hung the sheets on the inside of bathroom stalls all over campus, ensuring that most students would have ample time to "research" their representatives in local, state, and national government.

We also set up tables outside popular student hangouts, providing voter registration forms and encouraging students to vote for the environment. This system worked very well: many students were interested in voting, and now they had some concrete information to guide their decisions. Frequently students would stop at our table and ask, "Which candidate are you with?" While some were suspicious, many students seemed impressed that we hadn't been hired by a congressional campaign or a political party. Several people asked why we were doing this, and the truth was that it was because we cared about these issues.

In the end, we were able to register many people who said that they had never voted before. Voter turnout on campus that election increased by almost 20 percent, partially due to our efforts. All in all, both of my interests were satisfied during that fall, and without the strain on my voice.

MoveOn Tips

- Pick up voter registration forms from either the county seat or the League of Women Voters.

- For your registration drive, choose a topic to focus on that is broad but not necessarily well covered during the media blitz of elections.

- Go to www.fec.gov/votregis/vr.htm to print out copies of the National Voter Registration form, which is good in most states (see the site for details).

- Research the candidates' voting stances and records at places like www.vote-smart.org or www.opensecrets.org. List the information you find in a format that is easy to read.

- Post your information in public restrooms, local coffee shops, or any other community gathering space. As long as information is nonpartisan, most places are willing to have it posted.

Terrill Legueri was born and raised in Colorado and attends Grinnell College in Iowa.

Get Your Office to Vote

Kelly Holmes, 25, Austin, Texas

In the fall of 1999, I was attending the University of Texas at Austin and working at a local company. For the first time, I had "fallen in love" with a presidential candidate, and I became involved with the University Democrats chapter. At one meeting, an employee of the Voter Registrar's Office deputized us all as volunteer deputy registrars.

In order to register voters in Texas, you have to be deputized as a registrar—so this set me on an important campaign to register and remind others to vote. I got the idea to have a voter registration drive at my workplace. About 1,000 employees at my company in Austin weren't being reminded to register to vote before the 30-day deadline in Texas or to vote in upcoming elections. Surely now that I was oozing Official Voter Registrar Power, I could help remedy the situation!

I contacted someone I knew in the Human Resources department and pitched my idea to him. I would place registration card collection boxes in our building; I'd pick up the cards every few days and deliver them to the Voter Registrar's Office downtown. We would send an email to all employees in Austin explaining the collection boxes and the deadline for registering to vote. Then we'd send another email when early voting and Election Day came near.

Not only did he agree to do it, but he also was as excited as I was. All I'd had to do was initiate the conversation.

Four years later, my company has grown into three large buildings in Austin, and I'm still organizing voter registration drives and sending reminders about upcoming elections. If I ever doubt the value of what I'm doing, I just have to think of all the people who wouldn't have registered or voted had it not been for my reminders.

MoveOn Tips

- Find out your state's laws about registering voters. You may or may not need to be deputized.

- Get the support of your employee relations or human resources department. Offering employees a short time off to go vote is a great, socially responsible perk.

- Email employees about registration deadlines, early voting periods, and election dates. If you have time, walk from office to office (or cube to cube) with voter registration cards. If people aren't registered, offer to wait while they fill out the card and to turn it in for them (unless your state has laws against this).

- Make sure all communication about voting is nonpartisan to avoid offending anyone.

- Tell voters about some nonpartisan resources where they can learn more about the election. Try www.vote-smart.org. In addition, the League of Women Voters, www.lwv.org, has state and local chapters that can help.

- Post reminder flyers in elevators, restrooms, and break rooms.

- Get supplies, such as registration forms, at the office of your local voter registrar (or equivalent).

- On Election Day, organize a voting lunch. Email an invitation to go vote and then eat lunch. Have people RSVP, so you can make reservations and so they'll be more likely to actually come.

- For each person who brings in an "I Voted" sticker the day after an election, offer a reward, such as a donut or a muffin. No matter what you offer, this really works.

Kelly Holmes is a technical writer who lives with her partner, Erik, her dog, Molly Brown, and her cat, Shadow.

Maximize the Vote on Election Day

Skip Robinson, 64, Santa Rosa, California

I first learned precinct organizing in November 1962, two years after John F. Kennedy was elected president. I was finishing college at the University of Illinois, and I deeply wanted to support what he was trying to do. I thought that working locally to get voters out for the congressional election would be a good and practical place to start.

I was a bit anxious because I knew nothing about the art of precinct organizing; but I also felt very excited because I had found a way to help. I was looking forward to learning more about our political process.

There was a long tradition in central Illinois of systematic Democratic precinct work. Using educated volunteers, the party aimed to get virtually every eligible voter to vote on Election Day. The precinct I lived in needed work, and I volunteered to develop it. I immediately found out that the precinct was just 250 or so voters in my immediate neighborhood, with fixed boundaries and a nearby neighborhood voting place.

My first job was to get an official printed precinct list from the county voter registration office. As I looked it over, I found that the list was organized by streets and addresses in the precinct, with party designation after the voter's name (there, it was Democrat, Republican, Independent, or DS, meaning decline to state). Most had given their phone numbers when they registered and had allowed the numbers to be listed, as well.

I began to say howdy to my precinct neighbors by phoning and by walking the nearest blocks and knocking on some doors. I was looking for anyone who would be willing to call others, make political signs, have signs in their yards, make packets of material for people going door-to-door, give people rides to the polls on Election Day, be poll "watchers" on Election Day, and the like. To my delight, people were generally quite nice on the phone and at the door. A number offered to help, and several offered to share the job of calling those in the precinct. Some offered to walk to neighbors' houses in their blocks. Soon there were enough callers sharing the job to call the whole precinct and to visit everyone on each block.

As election time approached, each of the volunteers became more involved, and more people decided to help. Election Day dawned with a whole precinct team ready to maximize turnout. Many volunteers across the precinct had not met each other before, and I have been pleased to find that some formed strong, lasting friendships. Personally, I found some of my best friends during that campaign (and they lived right nearby).

At the next major election, when Barry Goldwater tried to take the presidency, our team was ready to help bring out the vote to say "No!" (We aimed for 100 percent turnout and came delightfully close.)

I'm getting ready to call the county elections office to get the contact list for the precinct where I now live. If there was ever a time to get involved, maximize the vote, and preserve our beloved democracy, it is now.

MoveOn Tips

- The entire country is divided into geographical precincts, each with about 250 to 500 potential voters. To receive a precinct list—which includes the name, address, party affiliation, and in most cases a phone number of the registered voters in your neighborhood—simply call your county or local government offices for the Elections Department.

- Set up a precinct website on which you can put key information, help coordinate work to be done, and facilitate communication among precinct workers.

- Despite the new "don't call" lists, political phone campaigning is still allowed. Don't hesitate to call those in your precinct and enlist their pledges to vote on Election Day.

- Different people like to do different things. Allow volunteers to help in ways they feel most comfortable.

Dr. Skip Robinson is a lecturer at Sonoma State University and teaches psychology of conflict resolution internationally. He is also a consultant, a writer, and increasingly a retiree.

Make a Personal Request to Nonvoters

Elise Davies, 42, Port Hueneme, California

I was having lunch with my daughter, Annemarie, and I had a mission—to get her to register to vote. She's 23 this year and has never voted because she believes that our political system is a joke, all politicians are crooked, and voting doesn't change anything.

This wasn't the first time I'd tried to get her to vote, but this time was different. It was about the survival of the last shreds of civil rights we've got left. It was about saving our country and our world from a small group of people who are hell-bent on world domination at any cost. This time I wasn't going to let it go.

Annemarie is no pushover, though, so I needed a strategy. I planned to talk to her about issues that she could relate to. I started with the conservative threat to *Roe v. Wade*, the Supreme Court case protecting the right to abortion. She listened politely. Then I moved on to the abortion gag rules the administration has enacted so that they never actually have to give money toward defeating AIDS overseas, and how I feel this conservative administration doesn't give a damn about women's rights.

I still wasn't making much progress, and I was getting desperate, so I did what up until that minute I thought was the unthinkable—I asked her to register and vote in the primary as a favor to me. Finally she agreed. She would do it for me. Then I asked her, since she didn't seem to care who got elected, to vote for my candidate. OK, she said, she'd do that as well. For one last favor, I asked her to get all her friends who don't vote to register. And she agreed to do that too!

The amazing thing about this story for me is that when I received the general call from MoveOn for story submissions for this book, I wistfully read the email, thinking how great it would be if I had a good story of activism to share with others. It never occurred to me how significant my action was until I told my sister while we were chatting one day. That's really the important message here: The little things we do *are* truly significant and do make a difference.

Now I make it a habit to ask every friend I know who doesn't vote to do it for me. It's probably one of the best gifts I can receive from them, and I let them know it. I'm sending a care package to my niece at college with voter registration cards and flyers for my candidate, so she can hand them out on campus. And today I went to lunch with a co-worker and asked him to vote as a favor to me. Get outta my way—I'm on a roll!

MoveOn Tips

- Give your friends and family extra incentive to vote by holding an Election Day party or dinner to watch the returns. On the invitation, you can say something like, "Come join us after you've voted, to share the ups and downs of Election Night with friends." Have favors or small door prizes, and try to make it something people look forward to every year.

- Include your children in the election process by taking them with you when you vote and then inviting them to the Election Night festivities. Some people make up "scorecards" to help kids (and even adults) keep track of the returns. It's never too early to impart how important it is to vote.

Elise Davies is an executive assistant and mother of three. She became politically active with the onset of the illegal war on and subsequent occupation of Iraq.

Participate in a Phone Bank

Susan Truax, 43, El Segundo, California

As the working mother of three growing boys, I consider it a great day when our family has been fed, cleaned, educated, exercised, and loved. With kids at three schools, clients to please, an active volunteer schedule, and a husband who has all the same responsibilities, great days require keen organizational skills.

I have fleeting fantasies of becoming a more engaged, informed, responsible citizen once my everyday obligations have been met—but of course those obligations are relentless. Then an event happened in California that spurred me to action. I watched in stunned disbelief as a petition to recall the governor was assembled, scrutinized, and approved. I was shocked when early polls showed that the majority of Californians favored recalling Gray Davis. How could this be? Couldn't my fellow voters see that this vote wasn't about whether or not we liked the governor but rather about the lack of justification for the recall campaign? Hadn't he just been elected by a majority of voters? That I was not among them was entirely beside the point. This was about protecting the democratic process!

How could one work-from-home public relations consultant make a difference in a statewide campaign? I wanted to do my part, but defeating an unjustified gubernatorial recall (read: saving democracy) is a big thing to have on your to-do list during back-to-school season. Enter MoveOn.

MoveOn sent me regular email updates keeping me informed and offering suggestions on ways I could defeat the recall at home in my spare time. I began my personal campaign against the recall by forwarding MoveOn petitions and messages to a group of family, friends, and co-workers.

Closer to the election I became one of MoveOn's phone bank volunteers. Assuming responsibility for calling my first list of 20 voters was a challenge that made me feel I was part of history in the making. Enthused, I signed up to contact another set of names, then another. I got pretty good at pronouncing the tough names, and, before long, it didn't sound like I was reading my message. I had a running contest with myself to see how many people I could reach in 15 minutes. The boys overheard my spiel so often, they entertained us with their own humorous versions of my get-out-the-vote script.

I may have served a few late dinners in those weeks leading up to the recall election, but I also set a good example for our kids about standing up for beliefs. Regardless of the election's outcome, I knew I had done my part in the effort to defeat the recall.

As a volunteer with MoveOn, I made 380 calls to registered voters. I spoke to nice people, the vast majority of whom claimed not to support the recall. Perhaps that explains why I was so surprised when the election was called only moments after the polls closed.

The governor was out. The Terminator was in. Was October 7, 2003, a great day? Well, at least the kids were fed! Soon after I crawled out of my hole of political depression, I took comfort in knowing I had worked with hundreds of MoveOn volunteers toward a common goal—at home, in my spare time.

MoveOn Tips

- Volunteer for phone banks by contacting local organizations with which you have an affinity. You can sign on for as few as 20 numbers at a time, taking on more only as you have the time.

Susan Truax is a public relations consultant to technology, consumer, and education clients. She has received the Dave Jones Award, given by the El Segundo Chamber of Commerce for outstanding volunteer service and dedication to education, and the Outstanding Volunteer of the Year Award from the El Segundo Unified School District.

III: The Many Faces of the Media

Introduction

David Fenton, CEO, Fenton Communications

"If you don't like the news, go out and make your own" is a saying coined by a San Francisco radio personality in the late 1960s.

That's what MoveOn members do. How refreshing, and how important in this time when the media are more shallow and sensational than ever.

These days, diverse viewpoints are narrowed by both the corporate concentration of media ownership and the cultural proclivities of media that would rather cover Britney Spears than global warming. Today, the Right successfully dominates media outlets and thought itself.

In this climate, MoveOn members call press conferences, write letters to editors, monitor and respond to media bias, work on media reform legislation, alert reporters to important stories they haven't covered, submit op-ed columns to newspapers, develop their own programs on public access TV, and contribute funds for TV and print advertising designed to stimulate coverage of the progressive agenda.

This chapter contains tips from members on how they do all these activities. It's a primer for media activism.

Active we must be. We can't have an educated citizenry, or a real democracy, if the Jeffersonian idea of a diverse, free press isn't realized. And it won't be without citizen activism to keep corporate media decision makers on their toes.

It's bad enough that we live in a country where no thought is allowed to last longer than 8 seconds—the length of the average TV sound bite now—unless, that is, one has enough money to buy the whole 30 seconds of a TV ad. No wonder Americans think that Saddam Hussein was behind 9/11 and that George Bush is improving Medicare. No wonder demagoguery trumps complexity.

And no wonder people in the rest of the world, especially Europe and Japan, know more and hold more progressive views than many Americans.

Their media treat subjects in depth. Their election campaigns are not reduced to 30-second ads.

The media are the problem; the Internet is part of the solution, empowering citizens across the country to keep media honest and to demand coverage of diverse views. This work is essential. Without the contributions of MoveOn members, we wouldn't be able to buy our own 30-second ads to unmask the Orwellian deception propagated by our nation's leadership.

Fenton Communications, the public relations and advertising company I run to help nonprofit public interest organizations get their messages heard, is privileged to be part of the MoveOn community. What a great sense of optimism comes over us when we get member feedback, ideas, and support.

After Barry Goldwater's defeat in 1964, conservative organizations gave priority to dominating the media. They have succeeded more fully than they thought possible. They bought radio and TV stations. They created think tanks to manufacture language and ideas. Over time, they succeeded in pressuring the mainstream media to move to the Right.

Progressive organizations are finally starting to build a serious movement to restore media balance. We are creating radio networks, purchasing stations, exposing media bias, aggressively placing spokespeople on television and radio, and buying advertising. MoveOn is playing a key role in this awakening. The pendulum is finally swinging, thanks to all of you.

Read More, Watch TV News Less

Kate Cox, 27, Astoria, Queens, New York

My father is a journalist. He has written for the same newspaper for 30 years. The children in my family were bred with a healthy respect for freedom of the press, as well as freedom of speech and expression. My parents taught us to view every issue with a critical eye and to analyze any given situation for truthful content, not merely sentiment. I have taken those lessons with me into the workplace, the community, and the voting booth.

On September 11, 2001, my critical eye was tested. While the mass media have always bombarded us with images of human suffering and injustice, for me, this was different. This was *my* city on fire. These were *my* friends and neighbors running for their lives. Any amount of desensitization I might have developed in the past was shattered in an instant. Like many people in this country, I was glued to my television set for weeks on end, watching images of the attacks on the World Trade Center and the Pentagon play over and over, while commentators tried to make sense of the events for us. I went to bed every night with a deeper and deeper sense of foreboding about what our world was quickly evolving into.

In nightly phone conversations with my father, I ran down the list of things I'd heard and seen on television that day that I found sad or terrifying. The nation was entering a very scary time, and I was firmly in the grip of intense fear and anxiety. Each night as I ended the conversations with my father, he said, "Remember, *read* more than you *watch*." In daily emails, he also urged me to start the day with a newspaper, instead of the morning news programs. He told me that limiting myself to a half hour of coverage per night would help me sleep better. My father reminded me that we are all incredibly susceptible to images and pictures, especially those set to softly touching music. If we allow ourselves to take all of our information from the footage we see on the nightly news, we lose sight of the truth in any given situation. We lose our ability to relate. We become uninformed. He told me that pictures tell only part of the story.

My father was right. I started to read everything I could get my hands on, from newspapers and magazines to social and historical commentary. I read articles and essays written by theologians, teachers, and scientists. I became a subscriber to several publications to ensure that I would always have information first, before images. Each time I sat down to read, my critical eye became more able to focus. I found a sense of perspective and learned to put world events into a historical context. For every essay that said the world was ending, there was one that said it was being rebuilt.

I slowly began to sleep better. I began to feel I had power in a situation that had previously made me feel powerless. I read about opportunities for participation and service, and I started to see myself as a vessel of peace and a force for change.

I am still deeply moved by the images of profound suffering and injustice I see in every corner of the world. I am still brought to tears each time I see footage of the collapse of the World Trade Center. I have learned, however, always to read what's behind the picture. There, I find hope, truth, and details. For me, there is healing in those details. Information is power.

MoveOn Tips

- In your search for information, include types of written material that you have not previously explored, such as published sermons, speeches, and essays.

- Read material featuring viewpoints that differ from yours politically, spiritually, or emotionally. This will help you see all sides of an issue.

- Limit your television viewing. Before tuning in, thoughtfully consider which programs will be most valuable to you in your personal search for information.

Kate Cox is an actress and co–artistic director of the not-for-profit theatre company This Woman's Work Theatre.

Write a Letter to the Editor

Jack Kennedy, 56, Nobleboro, Maine

I was already married and had an infant son when I graduated from Boston College in 1969. A few months earlier I had received my military draft notice. Although I had serious misgivings about the Vietnam War, I wasn't the protester type. When my country called, I answered by enlisting in the army's officer candidate program. Nine months later, at Fort Sill, Oklahoma, and only three weeks from graduation as an artillery officer, I came to the anguished decision that the war was impossible to justify. I filed as a conscientious objector. It was a rough time, but we survived, and I got an honorable discharge a year later.

After that experience, like many in my generation, I became disillusioned with government. For more than 30 years, I ignored politics. Then September 11, 2001, happened, and the country reacted with such fear that I could see we were headed for a new kind of cold war mentality. For a year I watched, with growing alarm at the new militarism and civil rights abuses. I joined MoveOn, signed petitions, and contributed $20 here and there to advertising campaigns.

Finally, on the first anniversary of 9/11, I felt compelled to speak up, and I wrote a letter to the editor, which was published in my three local papers. Every Sunday since, I have written a piece for the local paper. So far, 24 of my letters have been published, some as editorials. I also email them every Sunday night to my growing list of like-minded web friends.

I am still the same person I was in 1969. I'm not going to stand on a bridge with a sign, go to a rally, or walk door-to-door for a political candidate. All of my writing and contributing I do from my computer, sitting here in my pajamas on Sunday mornings in my little antique farmhouse in rural midcoast Maine. I know it's not much; I reach a few thousand people in my region with an alternative point of view about twice a month. But when I imagine there are others—thousands all over the country—writing, petitioning, and giving a few bucks here and there, well, then it becomes a big deal. And just maybe we can change the country a bit for the better.

Jack Kennedy is married to his childhood sweetheart, and they have two grown sons. He founded Jackeroos, an outlet for traditional handmade products of the Asia-Pacific region.

MoveOn Tips for Writing a Letter
Gary Porter, 57, Ann Arbor, Michigan

Over the years I have written many letters to the editor, and every letter I've sent has been published (although I realize this is not normally the case). Letters are a stunningly inexpensive way to influence hundreds, even thousands, of readers. I once wrote a letter published in the *Wall Street Journal,* which meant that it was delivered to more than a million readers. Following are the guidelines I go by in my own letter writing:

- Try to make the letter interesting and engaging. You can do this by having a subject "percolate" for a time. Make notes during the week as you think of things to say. Make statements in a clever way, as if you were talking to a friend.

- Write short, clear sentences that cover only one point.

- Follow the rules of the newspaper, especially about length.

- Make several revisions, to make sentences simpler and ideas clearer.

- Hold onto the letter for a day or two, and then give it a final touch-up before sending it out.

- As you follow the daily news, note statistics about subjects that are important to you.

- Use the Internet to double-check any pertinent facts or statistics.

- Adopt the formula I've used successfully: (1) an introductory topic sentence that defines your subject and engages the reader; (2) up to five specific points on the topic, each in a separate paragraph, that support your introductory sentence; (3) a conclusion, including a possible call to action.

Here's an annotated example of a letter on economic policy, using that formula:

Introductory sentence:
Many people in our society can no longer afford to live in it.

- If you're writing a letter about a specific situation that illustrates your point, try something like, "In July of this year Katish Roberts was forced to disenroll at Green Community College when her two-year-old son got pneumonia. Her story illustrates the fragility of the working poor in our society."

- Try to avoid introductory sentences like the following: "President Bush's economic policy really makes me upset." The reader would expect to see examples of when and how you are upset, e.g., "In the morning when I wake up," instead of examples of economic policy, which is the point of this introductory sentence.

Economic point in second paragraph:
The Census Bureau reports that 40 percent of households in our society earn an average of $10.12 per hour, or about $20,000 per year. After housing, food, and clothing are subtracted, these people cannot afford what most of us take for granted, including education, insurance, and health care.

- Note how this second sentence amplifies the primary sentence. It tells the reader the effect of the data on a segment of our society.

Another economic point in third paragraph:
The United States has the widest gap of any industrialized country between its rich and its poor. The richest 400 families in the United States now own roughly as much as the bottom 40 percent of families, 100 million people.

A broadening point in fourth paragraph, about how this hurts us all, not just the poor:

Latin American countries have shown for decades the problems that result when a wide gap exists between rich and poor. Problems in Latin American countries as a result of this gap include political instability, unclean water, poor roads, less chance for educational achievement, and national irrelevance.

Final paragraph, summing up the argument and providing a suggested action:

The wide gulf between rich and poor in the United States hurts us all. If we ignore this problem we cannot expect to remain prosperous. Vote for candidates in the next election who recognize this issue and will take steps to correct it.

Gary Porter is president of a firm engaged in electronic commerce. He has an M.B.A. from the University of Michigan and a B.A. in English.

Respond to Biased Reporting

Richard E. Chard, 38, Reston, Virginia

T he habit of certain media outlets and reporters to give their "as it should be" version of the news, rather than the "as it really is" version, has great impact on public opinion and election results. It's up to us, as consumers and citizens, to keep this practice in check and prod the media to be honest.

Over time I noticed one reporter for the *Washington Post* who seemed to consistently express his biases as if they were fact. In one instance in the spring of 2003, he wrote a story about how GOP strategist Karl Rove was drawing bigger crowds in New Hampshire than any of the Democratic presidential contenders. The reporter concluded that Rove's draw could only portend good things for Bush and bad things for Democrats, and that strong Republican support would be expected in New Hampshire, a state he said "Bush handily carried in 2000." As a native of New Hampshire, I sensed that these statements were not correct. I knew that Bush had not "handily" carried the state and that in fact Gore and Nader combined out-polled Bush by about 15,000 votes (3 percent of the votes cast).

Armed with the skills I'd garnered from my participation in MoveOn's Media Corps, I started checking around. The facts were dramatically different from what the *Washington Post* was reporting. True, the audience to see Karl Rove at St. Anselm's College was larger than the crowd for Dick Gephardt or John Edwards, but, as the *Concord Monitor* reported, about half of those in attendance were there to protest Bush's policies, not support them—a fact that was lost somewhere between Manchester and Washington. In addition, both Gephardt and Edwards had experienced the misfortune of blizzards on their campaign days at St. Anselm's, and even in New Hampshire people tend to stay off the roads in blizzard conditions.

On this and other issues, I contacted the ombudsman employed by the *Post* as a readers' advocate, especially in areas where reporters had violated the principles of journalism. Adhering to MoveOn's advice, I shared the facts above, entreating the *Post* to cease stating so-called facts without evidence to back them up. Soon after, I received a defensive email from the reporter, who informed me that his stories were not meant to be news but were instead analysis. I responded that, if this was true, he should be noting that distinction in his articles. Since then, his blatantly biased stories have had an "analysis" label on them, and the remainder of his stories have stopped stating conjecture and opinion as facts.

The media are indeed biased, but, if we speak up when the facts as they report them do not match the facts that we or others have observed, we can help neutralize the propaganda and get back to the reporting.

MoveOn Tips

- MoveOn's Media Corps runs an organized effort to watch the news and report on misinformation reported as news. Join to become active in making certain that the media adhere to the principles of journalistic integrity.

- Read your local newspaper as frequently as possible, and make a note when something doesn't sound right or when there is obvious false information. Then do some research using www.google.com or other online search engines to see if another source reported on the story in question and compare the assertions in each story.

- Use facts to request that your local paper report the news rather than opinion masquerading as news.

- Choose your battles. It's ineffective to become the "crank" who complains about every story, but you can save notes on a specific trend you see in your local media and then make a larger complaint.

- Let passion be your guide, and select an area in which you are interested as the focus of your media watch.

Richard E. Chard is currently a senior research associate at a Washington, DC, health care association. He received his Ph.D. in political science and statistics from Stony Brook University (State University of New York) in 1998.

Alert the Media to Uncovered Events

Mary Rickard, 51, Chicago, Illinois

As a publicist, I've been acutely aware that the number of media outlets and the amount of news coverage on local issues have been in steady decline during the past decade. At first, I assumed this was merely the result of reduced advertising revenues and the consequence of larger media absorbing smaller TV stations and newspapers. I didn't see the full picture until I received a bulletin from MoveOn in the fall of 2002, describing the causes and conspiracy of media consolidation.

I hadn't realized that in the past 20 years, control of the worldwide media had been reduced from 50 corporations to only 6 worldwide conglomerates. These 6 now own all the major television networks, radio stations, magazines, cable TV stations, film and music studios, and newspaper chains. Once I realized how drastic the situation was, I became fascinated and searched all the related websites, including www.fair.org, www. accuracy.org, www.openairwaves.org, www.democraticmedia.org, www. takebackthemedia.com. I read articles and books by media pundits Robert McChesney and John Nichols, and I started to understand the dire implications for our democracy of current media trends.

In 2003, impending Federal Communication Commission (FCC) rulings threatened to raise the media ownership cap, endangering many more independent news outlets. This very important ruling would allow megaconglomerates to acquire even more media outlets in every market, further homogenizing the news. FCC Chair Michael Powell (son of Secretary of State Colin Powell) hoped to push this deregulation through without public announcement or comment, giving only a couple of months' notice.

I alerted the Publicity Club of Chicago (PCC), which then published a notice in its monthly newsletter about an independently organized FCC public forum. The next month, I submitted a newsletter article describing the FCC's plans. As the Senate vote on the FCC's deregulation neared, an alert was emailed to all members, encouraging them to contact their legislators to oppose the changes. Some concerned PCC members went to their other professional organizations to notify independent writers and journalists. I also emailed an alert to our network of local peace groups, informing thousands of Chicagoans of the proposed rulings and urging them to call their senators.

When Associated Press wrote the first major article on the FCC regulations in April 2003, I forwarded the online version to every community newspaper in Chicago and the suburbs. Since these rulings would affect small newspapers, I figured these smaller publishers would be motivated to take action. Some of them might even reprint the AP article.

When MoveOn produced an online bulletin summarizing the FCC legislation, I realized that the information would make a perfect press kit, containing all the necessary information for a journalist to write a story. I forwarded the entire document to a reporter I thought might be sympathetic and simply wrote, "Can you write about this?" He did not respond. Two weeks later, however, two feature articles appeared in the *Chicago Tribune* on the topic of media consolidation. Although the articles skirted issues that might be critical of the *Tribune,* they certainly explained the dangers to independent and locally produced media.

A couple of months later, when I heard Robert McChesney speak at Public Square, a nonprofit that runs salon-type discussion groups throughout Chicago, he said we needed an "army" of people to spread the word about the FCC rulings. I approached him afterward and suggested that he enlist the support of the Public Relations Society of America (PRSA) in Washington, DC, the largest national association of public relations professionals in the country. Certainly they would understand. I emailed him the contact information, and a month later, PRSA sent press releases nationwide announcing the association's opposition to the FCC rulings.

FCC Commissioner Michael Powell encountered unexpected opposition from Congress and the public. A wave of protest considered unimaginable just months before prevented him from slipping these changes through. I was one of many people who had made a personal effort to spread the word. Powell was forced to conduct a public relations tour to generate support for his position.

The moral of my story is that one person with a computer and Internet access can help to inform and influence thousands. The cumulative effect of each of our actions—writing a couple of articles and forwarding others to the right people—can have a tremendous impact.

MoveOn Tips

- Pay attention to what stories are being covered—and neglected—in your local media.

- Notice which journalists are more dedicated to covering important and controversial issues.

- Call reputable journalists, and encourage them to cover an issue that you feel is being underreported.

- Present the background information and story angle in a format reporters can use. For example, provide them with a human interest story that illustrates the problem resulting from concentration of media ownership. These might include: nonprofits that can't get their message out, minorities whose concerns are underreported, environmental issues that don't get aired, or public school or transportation issues that are ignored.

- Access the news via email listservs such as www.truthout.org, www.democrats.com, and www.prwatch.org. Other good sites include www.salon.com, www.alternet.org, www.mediareform.net, and www.indymedia.org. Generally, the creators of these sites comb through the most important stories written nationally and internationally and compile them in daily or weekly lists.

- Every major newspaper and wire service also has an online edition where past articles are archived. Search these, and forward to journalists or media activists stories that were not covered or were misrepresented in the United States.

- Get the support of clubs, associations, and networks that might care about your cause.

- Never underestimate the impact a single person can have.

Mary Rickard has been actively involved with MoveOn for almost two years. She is an independent marketing/PR professional with a specialization in issues management.

Place an Ad

Greg Nees, 54, Longmont, Colorado

On Sept 13, 2001, I was trying to come to grips with the shocked numbness I felt after the attack on the World Trade Center. I meditated on the horror and suffering of the victims and their families and was overcome with grief. These feelings were almost unbearable, and they got worse when I realized that we were going to seek revenge. Thousands more innocent people, who had nothing to do with the attack, were going to be killed. I saw the potential for a cycle of violence and I had to do something.

I wanted to write to President Bush *urging* restraint and caution, but I was convinced that my letter would never make it through the bureaucratic filters. Still, this idea would not leave me in peace, so I sat down at my computer and began typing out the letter. It was a moment of inspiration, and the words flowed easily. Within a few hours I was satisfied with my letter and mailed it off to the White House. As an afterthought I emailed it to a few friends.

The response to my emailed letter was overwhelming. It got forwarded to many thousands of people around the world. I had struck some deep chord, and I began getting positive letters from Europe, Africa, and Asia. I was astonished and gratified by these emails.

One woman from Japan, Yumi Kikuchi, wrote to ask if I would be willing to publish my letter as an ad in a major U.S. newspaper, and I agreed. Yumi, an environmentalist and mother of four, is a real force of nature and soon had a group of like-minded people organized. We called ourselves the Global Peace Campaign and began soliciting donations to have my letter published in the *New York Times*.

When I learned that full-page ads can cost more than $100,000, my doubts again came to the fore. That seemed to me an impossible sum to reach. But Yumi was determined, and the folks she called on for help were ready for a challenge.

The Global Peace Campaign sprang into life with help from organizers in Japan, Great Britain, Germany, and the United States. Soon we had a website and were in communication with Veterans for Peace, who were also counseling caution in our foreign policy and the need to understand the root causes of the WTC attack before instigating more violence.

Despite my doubts, with seemingly endless hours of work, the campaign moved forward and more money came in, mostly due to Yumi's determination and tireless efforts. To my great joy, my letter was published as a full-page ad in the October 9, 2001, edition of the *New York Times*.

The public's response was immediate and overwhelming. Calls came in from radio stations, newspapers, and TV stations for interviews, and suddenly I was getting a lot more attention than ever before in my life. For the next two months I dedicated most of my time and energy to dealing with those responses.

Since then, Yumi and others have moved forward with the Global Peace Campaign, and I am now a full member of Veterans for Peace. We continue to work for a peaceful world where all people are safe and have the basic necessities of life.

MoveOn Tips

- Make a contribution to an ad campaign for an issue you care about. Even small contributions add up and make a big difference. In late 2002, MoveOn asked members for $35,000 to place an ad in the *New York Times* that said "Let the Inspections Work." We were amazed when we raised $400,000 in less than a week, with the average contribution being $35. We ended up creating and running a TV and radio ad, posting billboard ads, and running ads in local newspapers. The press we got about these ads was also fabulous. Average citizens can support very effective media work when they join forces.

Greg Nees is a self-employed interculturalist. He helps people from different cultures understand one another better and work together cooperatively.

Reform the Media

Barbara Diamond Goldin, 57, Northampton, Massachusetts

After graduating from college and their ROTC programs, my daughter and son-in-law joined the army in May 2001. I had no inkling then that just two years later they would be serving our country as first lieutenants in Iraq, in separate locations due to wartime conditions.

Following media coverage of events became very important to me as a concerned and worried parent. But I felt increasingly frustrated trying to get the news. The sound bites on television did not fill me in on what I was hungry to know. What was really going on?

With the help of informed friends and family, I totally changed my media habits. I am now an avid radio listener, getting news from shows like *On the Media* and *Democracy Now*. From radio, newspapers, and Internet listservs, I get a more complete story, including the history of Iraq, the military strategy of the neoconservatives, and Defense Secretary Donald Rumsfeld's plans for the future of the army. I learn about the effect of depleted uranium and other health hazards on our troops—all of which affect my family personally. Information helps me cope with having my loved ones in Iraq, since I can't talk to them on the phone and can communicate only via sporadic brief emails and slow letters.

I began wishing it were easier for everyone to have access to unbiased, in-depth news coverage, and that's how I came to volunteer at the Free Press, an organization working for media reform. Each week for a couple of hours, I stuff envelopes, stick labels on flyers, delete obsolete email addresses—whatever job the organization needs done. I feel like I'm helping in this movement to give the public a voice in media regulation.

Thanks to the Free Press and MoveOn, I began to make phone calls and write letters to public officials. When I made my first call to a senator's office, I was petrified. I kept getting a busy signal, and when a human voice finally picked up, I forgot what I wanted to say, even though I had it written out in front of me. I managed to get out one squeaky sentence. Now I call easily and often about lots of issues.

In the weeks before the Federal Communication Commission (FCC) 2003 vote on media deregulation, I wrote letters to all five FCC commissioners, the White House, my two senators, and my congressional representative. I forwarded these letters to more than 50 friends and relatives and encouraged them to write their own letters. When I learned that the FCC and Congress had received more than 750,000 letters and emails against further media deregulation, I felt gratified that people were speaking out about who was really benefiting from this deregulation—the big media conglomerates, not the public.

Grassroots work can make a difference. Now, as worrisome as it is to have loved ones in Iraq, at least I know more about what's going on there. And here. Information helps me not feel totally in the dark and also helps me figure out what things I can do to promote the changes I want to see.

MoveOn Tips

- Keep a file of notes and articles about issues that concern you. You can draw on these when you write statements for calling or sending to your representatives.

- Sign up at www.MoveOn.org, the Free Press (www.mediareform.net), and other organizations. They email you updates about current media legislation, so you know when to contact your representatives. These groups provide contact information, the bill or resolution number, and a sample script you can use on the phone until you feel comfortable improvising.

- Write down what you want to say to your representatives before you call. You'll most likely get an aide, not the legislator, but a tally of callers' views will be given to the elected official.

Barbara Diamond Goldin is a writer and librarian.

Make Your Own Media

Cirilo Juarez, 43, Los Angeles, California

Not long ago, at a forum for peace, I saw the video *What I've Learned about U.S. Foreign Policy.* It was a real shocker. A discussion followed, and one thing that struck me was that several people talked about the lack of media coverage and the media's spin on things. The host said that we should be our own media. At that moment I decided to take the bull by the horns.

I knew that there was a medium known as public access TV, but, since I don't have cable or satellite TV, it was a case of "out of sight, out of mind" regarding political use of it—until that moment.

I remembered that, when I was part of an AIDS group, we had actually aired a show about AIDS on public access TV, although I was not part of that phase of the group's work. I also remembered that I'd been wanting to promote the Bus Riders' Union (of which I've been a member since 1996), and this was my big chance.

I didn't know where to begin, who to contact, or how to get started, but I knew I wanted to access the airwaves even on a small scale (the broadcast range for these stations is limited to a few small cities). I asked around and found out that you simply call your local city hall (in my case Whittier City Hall). You ask for the public or community TV access program or department, and you go from there. I did just that.

The people at city hall sent me to a high school campus in Hacienda Heights where the TV studio was. I obtained necessary information from the studio director, and I signed up on the spot over the phone to get started.

In late August, I went to an orientation meeting for the workshop for public access TV. It was exciting—I would learn how to be the producer /director of my own show. A workshop continues for six sessions, and when I complete it I will earn my video production certification.

I have my show already planned. It's called *Get on the Bus,* and it's a program with purpose and meaning. Its main focus is the Bus Riders' Union—its history, struggle, strategy, and accomplishments. The video will tell about racism in transportation policy in Los Angeles and will include other community issues. It will touch on political events and concerns, local, national, and world, both as information and as topics for debate. I'll also include musical talent, provided it has social change content or is political.

TV production sounds so monumental—but it's not. You'd be surprised how simple it really is. Like everything else, once you learn, it's easy. Operating a camera is pretty basic and uncomplicated. One show I helped to shoot has now aired, and that was exciting to see—my name in the credits.

I'm still in the certification process. Through the workshop I'm learning about lighting, editing, shooting, and the like. I'm getting hands-on experience and will shoot a small clip. Once that happens, I can submit my proposal for a show.

In my opinion, public/community access TV provides a great opportunity to bring out voices and images that the mainstream media won't touch. You too can be heard. Go for it.

MoveOn Tips

- First and foremost, be clear that you have a message, thought, or political point of view that you feel needs to get out.
- Decide how you want to present your message. Do you want comedy or theatre as your medium, a debate forum, a presentation of facts, figures, statistics?
- Create a catchy name for your show (something that arouses curiosity).
- Call your city hall (local municipality) to ask about public or community access TV and how to become a part of it. Say that you want to produce your own show.
- If the city has a production training program, jump on it and stick with it. You might be able to earn a certification, which could lead to paid work.
- Give your project time and dedication.

- Ask for help! No one does it alone. Talk with local organizations that might want to participate in your show. Build community.

- Remember the United Farmworkers' Union slogan: *Si, Se Puede!* (Yes, We Can!)

Cirilo Juarez is a migrant from Mexico who became a U.S. citizen in 1988 and has been a political activist ever since. He has been an active member of the Bus Riders' Union since 1996 and serves professionally as an escrow officer and notary signing agent.

Write an Op-Ed Piece

Elise Woods, 62, Hedgesville, West Virginia

Each year our local daily newspaper selects eight writers from the community to serve as columnists. Those selected agree to write an article every four weeks for the op-ed page. When I saw the notice about this in the paper, I knew that I needed to apply. I definitely had some things to say.

When I was selected to be a community columnist, the editorial staff told me that I could write about anything that had my attention. The first column I wrote was a kind of "toe in the water" introduction of myself to readers. As I wrote the piece, I noticed I felt vaguely uncomfortable. I realized it was a fear of being exposed to the scrutiny of others. Perhaps they would judge my ideas and find them lacking or simply wrong. Or they might vehemently disagree and want me to quit writing. Though I was anxious about how readers would respond, I decided that I just had to get over worrying about what anybody thought and say what I had to say.

Shortly after my first column appeared in print, I went to the big peace march in Washington, DC, on January 18, 2003. I knew that my February column was going to be about my experience of the march. I also knew that a sizable portion of the local population leaned toward supporting the military without asking questions about what else might be possible. The newspaper I write for has a long-running series on unsung heroes of wars past, and it's pretty conservative in its news reporting. So when I sat down to write about my experience and the reasons I participated in the march, I realized I had to write so that the reader could see the march through my eyes and hear it through my ears. I didn't want the piece to be judgmental or condemning of actions or policies, which I believe only serves to alienate people.

I wrote from my heart and exposed myself more than I thought possible. I talked about my motivation for going and described the experience of being with so many others, literally and figuratively facing in the same direction. I spoke of not being in agreement with everything I saw and heard, and then I waited for the response.

Only one reader wrote to me about that column. He said he completely disagreed with me but he would totally defend my right to say everything I had said. What a surprise! Not a single angry comment from anybody. Perhaps it had something to do with letting myself be exposed.

Recently I was walking to the post office when a woman I've never seen before crossed the street in front of me. She greeted me by name (she recognized me from the picture published with my columns) and told me that she and her husband read all of my columns. She wanted me to know how much they appreciate what she called "a refreshingly different viewpoint." I thanked her and went on my way, smiling.

MoveOn Tips

- When writing op-ed articles or letters to the editor, take responsibility for what you believe and present it in a personal way that the reader can relate to, even if he or she disagrees.

- Don't try to change others' mind. They have to do that themselves.

- Keep your writing tight, and get someone else to read your article or letter before you submit it.

- Remember that you're talking to real people when you write, even if you never meet them in person.

- Send your piece to more than one newspaper, if you wish, but let the papers know that others are also considering your piece. Multiple submissions can spur a paper to move quickly and print a piece, since that paper wants to be the first to publish it.

- Follow-up calls are critical. Papers receive hundreds of submissions and have limited space. When you call, make the case that your piece is a relevant, insightful look at an issue the papers' readers are interested in. Answer the question, Why is this piece newsworthy?

- If you get critical or angry responses to your work, don't take them personally.

- When a newspaper prints an op-ed piece, as opposed to a letter to the editor, your work appears as a columnist's viewpoint. Newspapers often print guest columns on their editorial pages when the subject matter is relevant. See whether your newspaper prints guest columns or op-ed pieces on its editorial page, and submit a column on a timely subject.

Elise Woods is co-owner of Business Technology Source in Shepherdstown, West Virginia. She has been writing off and on since high school.

Start a Political Book Club

Karen Bouris, 35, Makawao, Hawai'i

My book club's most heated and lively discussion occurred after we read a book that examined the economics of motherhood and child care. All five of us were professionals who had young children. The book struck a nerve in each of us, and we were eager to discuss the thoughts and feelings it raised. Two women had highlighted their books, marking each point they wanted to discuss. Only one of us had not completely finished the book—she had just given birth to her third child.

What was normally a one- to two-hour discussion of the book and our lives turned into a late-night debate on Social Security credits for stay-at-home parents, taxation, and child care subsidies. We discussed the Family and Medical Leave Act, politicians aware of family issues, and our experiences in the workplace as women with children. Like most mothers, we generally valued sleep above all else. But this book club meeting ran until 11:30 P.M., on a weeknight no less.

Books are powerful teachers. Nonfiction has quenched my curiosity about political issues and exposed me to a host of ideas and information. Novels have given me a deeper understanding about many things, from the struggles of new immigrants to 19th-century labor unions. In the pages of books, I have found myself in northern Africa witnessing unimaginable female "rites of passage," I have toured beef processing plants in the Midwest, and I have been shown evil in the camps at Dachau. I once had a book group that wanted to read only happy books, and it felt similar to wanting to acknowledge and drive through only the "nice" parts of town. The people in the group didn't want to know about the unkempt, troubled neighborhoods. But troubled areas and times do exist, even if they don't directly touch our neighborhoods or our lives. Books can introduce us to them, provide a torchlight, and guide us to understand another reality—both the beautiful and the ugly. They can inspire passionate debate among friends, knock us out of our television stupor, and propel us into responsible action.

My book group's discussion turned into action: it moved me so much that I wrote a book for couples on how to create intentional and equal parenting roles; it opened many group members' eyes to such financial issues as the need for long-term financial planning for part-time workers; and it spurred newfound dedication to examining public policies that support a variety of parenting and child care scenarios. This particular book and discussion changed the course of my life. Books do make a difference.

MoveOn Tips

- Start a book group that specifically focuses on political nonfiction and fiction. It's a great way to create dialogue and spark action.

- Set the tone and mission of the group early. You may want a group that explores a variety of political issues or one that focuses on a particular issue.

- Designate a skilled and tactful facilitator to keep the conversation dynamic, balanced, and respectful.

- Remind participants that every person's point of view has merit, because it comes from that individual's own experience. Try to listen and understand one another's reality.

- To find worthwhile books that explore political and social issues, use a bibliography, such as the annotated list in *Make a Difference*, by University of California, Berkeley, Professor Arthur Blaustein. Here is a short sampling of the novels he includes:

  Bastard out of Carolina by Dorothy Allison
  Another Country by James Baldwin
  The Memory of Old Jack by Wendell Berry
  The House on Mango Street by Sandra Cisneros
  Love Medicine by Louise Erdrich
  Mean Spirit by Linda Hogan
  The Rain God by Arturo Islas
  Ironweed by William Kennedy

The Woman Warrior by Maxine Hong Kingston
Bone by Faye Ng
My Year of Meats by Ruth L. Ozeki
Machine Dreams by Jayne Anne Phillips

Karen Bouris is the associate publisher at Inner Ocean Publishing and the author of *Just Kiss Me and Tell Me You Did the Laundry: A Couple's Guide to Negotiating Parenting Roles.*

MoveOn's Suggested Media Sources

Online

- Google News (http://news.google.com)
- Common Dreams (www.commondreams.org)
- Salon (www.salon.com)
- Alternet (www.alternet.org)
- Tom Paine (www.TomPaine.com)
- ZNet (www.zmag.org)
- Independent Media Center (www.IndyMedia.org)
- Free Press's News Headlines (www.mediareform.net)
- The Daily Howler (www.dailyhowler.com)
- Progress Report (www.americanprogress.org)
- FAIR (Fairness and Accuracy in Reporting) (www.fair.org)
- MediaChannel's Media Savvy listserv(ww.mediachannel.org)
- Truth Out (www.truthout.org)
- Free Speech TV (www.freespeech.org)

Radio

- National Public Radio (www.npr.org)
- Pacifica Radio (www.pacifica.org)
- Alternative Radio (www.alternativeradio.org)

Magazines and Newspapers

- *Christian Science Monitor* (www.csmonitor.com)
- *Mother Jones* (www.motherjones.com)
- *The Economist* (www.economist.com)
- *The Nation* (www.thenation.com)
- *New York Times* (www.nytimes.com)
- *Washington Post* (www.washingtonpost.com)
- *The Week* (www.theweekmagazine.com)

World News

- BBC News (http://news.bbc.co.uk)
- World News Network (www.wnnetwork.com)
- World Newspapers (in English) (www.worldnewspapers.com)
- *International Herald Tribune* (www.iht.com)
- *Guardian* (www.guardian.co.uk)

More to Read

- Opinion Pages, a collection of searchable editorials, opinions, and commentaries from hundreds of newspapers and magazines (www.opinion-pages.org)

- Diplomacy Monitor, a resource that tracks online diplomatic communiqués, press briefings, and related official documents worldwide in several languages (http://diplomacy monitor.com)

- The History Channel, a source for U.S. and international speeches (www.historychannel.com/speeches)

IV: Political Action Is Personal

Introduction
Nancy Pelosi, House Democratic Leader

Having served in the U.S. House of Representatives for 16 years, I know from firsthand experience that there is no voice more eloquent to members of Congress than that of their own constituents. Communicating with your elected officials—writing, calling, faxing, emailing, and meeting with your representatives and senators—is an essential, vital part of our democratic system. You are our bosses. We want and need to hear what you have to say.

I am blessed to represent most of the city of San Francisco. San Francisco has a long history of passionate political activism, and that tradition continues to this day. The huge volume of correspondence my office receives each week reflects my district's standing as one of the most active in the country. I am so fortunate to have the benefit of my constituents' views. Your members of Congress deserve the same.

As the essays in this chapter clearly illustrate, your representatives and senators will listen and respond. They may not always agree with you—and you may not be able to change their positions when they don't—but they want to know your views. That is why I am so pleased to see the activism that MoveOn has helped to generate, bringing everyday Americans back into politics.

Part of what makes our country great is the beautiful diversity of our citizens and the diversity of our views. But if we do not express our views, we deny the national debate the benefit of our experiences and opinions. We deny ourselves the opportunity to contribute to a better future for everyone.

Each generation has a responsibility to make the future better for the next. Every one of us has an individual responsibility to do our part. How we make our contribution to a better future is a personal decision.

The poet Percy Bysshe Shelley once wrote that the greatest force for moral good is imagination. With the problems facing our country, we need all the imagination we can muster: Imagination to think in new ways. Imagination to put ourselves in others' shoes and see things from a different point of view. Imagination to take a risk and become an active part of the democratic process. Imagination to create a society where all of us can reach our full potential.

We need new ideas in our society. We need new ideas in Congress. And the best source of fresh thinking is a fresh pair of eyes—your eyes, inspired by imagination.

Know thy power. Call, write, fax, email, or meet with your representatives and senators. Make your views known. Share your ideas and your imagination. Make certain a diversity of views is represented at the table. Only then can we make the future brighter and better for generations to come.

Write Letters to Congress That Work

Ari Melber, 23, Seattle, Washington

I got my first letter from an elected official when I was nine years old. At the time, I did not realize that my words would eventually reach the mayor's office. I was only focused on connecting with a single voter: my dad.

Seattle's mayoral election would not normally have interested me, but my parents were arguing about who was the better candidate, and I wanted to be a part of the action. I decided to throw my weight behind my mother's choice, Norm Rice. I used Magic Markers to make small signs that resembled those I had seen in the neighborhood. I scrawled "NORM" in thick, loopy letters and added my own catchphrases. Then I carefully placed the little posters on my dad's place mat before dinner.

Both my parents were impressed when they saw my political handiwork, but my dad could not be swayed. Even my finale sign—Norm. Norm. He's Our Man!—missed its mark. My parents dutifully went to the polls that night and canceled out each other's votes.

A few days later, my mom told me that Norm had won. She did not tell me, however, that she had sent my signs to his new office. So I was shocked when, a few weeks later, Norm Rice sent me a personal letter.

Except for the week before my birthday, I had never received mail from anyone, let alone a mayor. Norm thanked me for my efforts and playfully asked, "Where were you during my campaign?" I was completely psyched. I put that letter in plastic and showed it to everyone I knew.

Thirteen years later, I got a job reading the letters that people write to their representatives. Working as a legislative correspondent in the U.S. Senate, I read thousands of letters. Some people share stories and hopes, some advocate policies, and others list their frustrations.

Many constituents ask if their letters are making a difference. "Is anyone listening?" they want to know. While a single letter rarely sways a legislator, several dozen people's letters supporting the same policy can definitely make an impact, especially if they are about a small, specific action.

My family has always discussed public affairs, so I'd probably still be in politics today without the mayor's letter of thanks. But it spurred my interest and showed me that politics is about the connections and disagreements between real people. Unlike some of my peers, I saw our democracy as tangible, accessible, and exciting. I have worked in political advocacy for two years, and the letter from Mayor Rice remains one of my favorite breakthrough interactions.

MoveOn Tips

- To be most effective, write an individual letter, rather than copying a form letter.

- Begin with a clear objective, and show knowledge of the issue. Give personal experiences if you can. For example:

  "I urge you to support the full 6 percent increase in education funding for disadvantaged schools this year. As you know, Title I funding is critical for schools in poor neighborhoods, like Emerson Middle School in Johnson County. I know Emerson teachers who don't even have enough books for all their students . . ."

- If you've had past contact with the office or staff, mention it in the letter.

- Write from your heart. If you can, inject humor or unusual material in your letter. People have different styles, and there is no single correct format, but, an offbeat or heartfelt letter sometimes gets noticed and passed up the line more quickly.

Ari Melber served as a legislative aide for education and foreign policy in the U.S. Senate. He also worked as a field organizer in Iowa during the 2004 presidential campaign.

Talk to the Officials You Didn't Elect

Caryl Bigenho, 66, Simi Valley, California

In 1999 my husband and I were planning a trip to Washington, DC, for a family wedding. We decided to stay over for a few days to visit the capitol, so before leaving California we called the office of our congressperson, Elton Gallegly, to arrange for tickets to the House of Representatives.

During the conversation, we were asked if we would like a special "insider's" tour of the capitol and some time to talk with our representative. Since Gallegly is a very conservative Republican, we wondered what we could possibly discuss with him. But because we had the opportunity, we decided to try anyway.

Our visit coincided with the Jubilee 2000 campaign, a worldwide effort to reduce the debts of highly indebted poor countries around the world. Often these nations were expected to spend most of their country's income just to pay the interest on their debts. At that time a bill was before the House that would partially erase the debts of some of the impoverished countries. We decided to bring this issue to his attention.

We researched the bill online before leaving home. In Washington, we went to the Jubilee 2000 office to get more information and to pick up literature about the issue. Thus armed, we went to Capitol Hill for our tour and visit.

After our private tour, we were escorted into the representative's office. We spent a few minutes getting acquainted. Then he asked us if we had any issues of special concern. We told him we were interested in how he planned to vote on the bill for reducing the debts of the highly indebted poor countries. He told us he was unfamiliar with the legislation, and asked us to tell him more about it.

We told him about the legislation, and gave him copies of the information we had picked up at the Jubilee 2000 office. He thanked us for bringing it to his attention and told us he would have one of his aides research the issue. Later, he voted for the bill, and it passed.

Elected officials can easily be overwhelmed by the huge number of bills put before them each session. They rely on aides and constituents to research issues and keep them informed. They don't always get information on every piece of legislation. Even if your representatives have different political leanings from yours, you can still direct their attention to the issues you care about. Whether you voted for them or not, they're in office to serve as your representative.

MoveOn Tips

- Make an appointment for time with the official. Most have office time available in your local area, so a trip to Washington, DC, or your state capital isn't always necessary.

- If the official can't meet with you, an aide is a good substitute. Be sure you get to speak to someone who works with the types of issues that concern you.

- Do your homework before you go, and bring information about the issue to leave with the representative. Government publications are very effective because they are "official" information. The *Catalog of U.S. Government Publications* (www.gpoaccess.gov) provides an index to print and electronic publications created by federal agencies and a comprehensive list of official federal resources.

- Be polite, even if you seldom agree with the official. Follow up with a thank-you note that mentions the issue again. After the vote, if the legislator supported your position, write to say thanks again.

Caryl Bigenho retired after 30 years of teaching and counseling in the public schools of Los Angeles. She now writes about and advocates for environmental justice issues.

Support Clean Elections

Lola Boan, 73, Sun City, Arizona

After retiring as an elementary teacher, I became active in the League of Women Voters. The members of the Northwest Maricopa County League, most of whom are retired, have the time to watch state, local, and national government officials.

In 1996, with the encouragement of Nick Nyhart, executive director of the nonprofit Public Campaign, based in Washington, DC, various Arizona organizations and individuals interested in campaign finance reform at the state level formed a coalition, Arizonans for Clean Elections, to write a clean elections initiative. The primary goal of the clean elections movement is to help reduce the influence of big money in politics.

Under the proposed voluntary campaign finance system, participating candidates agree not to accept private campaign contributions except for contributions of "seed money"—not more than $110 per person—from individuals up to a total of about $2,500 for legislative candidates and $40,000 for governor. Candidates qualify for public funds by gathering a certain number of $5 contributions from individuals. Statewide candidates can obtain qualifying contributions only from within the state, and legislative candidates only from within their districts.

The revenue for the Clean Elections Fund comes from several sources: a surcharge on civil and criminal fines and penalties, contributions from individuals for which a matching tax credit can be claimed (up to a set amount), and the $5 qualifying contributions gathered by candidates.

Getting the necessary signatures for the Clean Elections Initiative in the heat of an Arizona summer was difficult, but many volunteers helped in this task. The initiative was placed on the 1998 ballot and won by a small margin. We were delighted!

Since the Clean Elections Initiative passed, it has encountered several court challenges, all unsuccessful. At this time, an initiative that would remove clean elections funding sources is being circulated and may appear on the 2004 ballot. However, the law is consistently popular with voters and candidates. A comparison of the Arizona statewide and legislative races in the 1998 and 2002 elections reveals that the number of candidates increased 24 percent; competition doubled for the state senate, both parties had full slates for statewide offices, and voter turnout increased 27 percent in the primary and 23 percent in the general election.

As other states and even global visitors have expressed interest in Arizona's Clean Elections Law, the League of Women Voters and other civic-minded organizations continue to work for universal, effective campaign finance reform. Unless this is achieved, our country will be dominated by special interest groups. This domination ultimately affects the average citizen by adversely influencing legislation on health care, environmental protections, education, media control, cost of consumer goods, and basic civil rights.

MoveOn Tips

- Get more information on clean elections at the Clean Elections Institute website, www.azclean.org, and at Public Campaign's website, www.publicampaign.org.

- Learn about starting an initiative or referendum, if your state provides this avenue for change, at www.iandrinstitute.org.

Lola Boan retired from teaching elementary school in 1995 and is an activist in civic affairs.

Volunteer for Campaigns

Michael A. Smith, 33, Kansas City, Missouri

S even to one: that's how much we were outspent. Impossible odds—and we beat them.

When Dr. Charles Wheeler announced his candidacy for the Missouri senate in 2001, few took him seriously. This former Kansas City mayor had been out of office for two decades. A practicing pathologist, he had focused his attention on his family and medical career after leaving the mayor's office. But a few volunteers believed that Dr. Wheeler's name recognition was still something special. The district was Democratic, so the general election was not a threat. Our challenge was to win the Democratic primary, in a field of three. Again and again, we were told it couldn't be done, that the city's political powers would line up behind someone else.

When the dust settled and the final candidates had filed for the senate seat, the political establishment had indeed coalesced around another candidate. An insider politician with ties to the city's powerful special interest lobbies, he quickly amassed money and endorsements. He hired the city's most feared consulting firm to run his political campaign. He saturated the district with direct mail and even ran commercials on cable TV. Our opponent spent $250,000 on the race. We spent $38,000, most of it raised in the last few weeks of the campaign. And we won.

While our opponent ran commercials and racked up endorsements, we stuck with yard signs. The signs, featuring a silhouette of our candidate and the word "integrity," brought memories of the years when he had served as mayor—years when the city actually seemed to be in the grip of somebody besides special interests and political consultants. Our single direct mail piece also stressed the integrity theme.

The first break finally came when the city's major daily newspaper endorsed Dr. Wheeler. According to the endorsement, the campaign theme, integrity, defined the election. Our leading opponent had lined up powerful special interests, but his own past was suspect: not only was he having tax problems, but he had even done time in jail for a check-kiting scheme.

My own job was to coordinate volunteers. We recruited people to talk to neighbors and supplied them with postcards. We wrote press releases and got our candidate out to every public forum we could find. We put yard signs on every corner in the parts of the district where our candidate was popular, in order to boost turnout. We knocked on doors, recruited more volunteers, and tried to create a presence in parts of the district where our candidate was less well known. In short, we used every low-cost method and volunteer we could find to stress a simple message: Our candidate has integrity, and he's back in politics.

On Election Day, Dr. Wheeler pulled off the upset, winning 48 percent to 41 percent, with 11 percent going to the third candidate. Grassroots politics had defeated the money, the special interests, and the endorsements.

MoveOn Tips

- Get behind a good, honest candidate.

- Develop a clear theme for the campaign.

- Be realistic, but don't let the conventional wisdom decide for you. Your candidate may have great name recognition throughout the city even without the high-level endorsements of the political establishment.

- Raise enough money to be competitive, but don't assume you have to outspend your opponent. Grassroots efforts really pay off! You'll need enough money to pay for yard signs, literature, newspaper advertisements, radio ads, a website, and so forth. But you can run a campaign on a shoestring if you build a base of committed volunteers with heart.

- Use volunteers to get out and meet voters. Sometimes volunteers are better than paid workers because citizens see that they believe what they say.

- When you volunteer in the campaign, choose the tasks that suit you: making phone calls, passing out leaflets, writing let-ters to the media, going door-to-door, registering voters, getting out the vote on Election Day, among others. Time com-mitment is up to you, and you can work at headquarters, at events, or even from home.

- Don't get discouraged. If we had $5 for every person who told us that it couldn't be done . . .

- Once you are a volunteer, find others to join you. It's a great way to be politically involved, meet people, and have fun.

- If you are overseeing volunteers, don't forget to keep them happy. Assign very clear roles and tasks, train them properly, and recognize their efforts.

Michael A. Smith is a visiting professor of political science at Kansas State University. He served as volunteer coordinator for the Wheeler for Senate Campaign and is author of *Bringing Representation Home,* a book about state legislators and their constituents.

Help Run a Campaign

Peggy Huppert, 45, Des Moines, Iowa

In 1997 I was busy working at my own consulting business and running a household that included three children, two dogs, and an attorney husband. My plate was more than full. I was active in politics, volunteering in campaigns and occasionally participating in Democratic party activities. But I had never led a campaign or taken any kind of a leadership role.

That all began to change when I took a trip to Washington, DC, with a group of under-40 Democrats called the 21st Century Forum. We're young professionals, mostly lawyers, who joined forces in 1995 with the encouragement of Iowa Senator Tom Harkin. Part of our trip included a meeting with Senator Harkin. He talked to us about what it would take to elect a Democratic governor in Iowa the following year, after 32 years of Republican rule. We were all from Polk County, the state's largest. Senator Harkin said bluntly, "The leadership of the Polk County Democratic party must change for us to win." We looked at one another and asked, "Who could do that?" He answered, "One of you."

That is what started me thinking about running for chair of the county party. When I returned home I started talking to people about it. Most discouraged me. The leadership was entrenched; several people had tried during the past ten years to unseat the chairs and fire the director, and it was they who found themselves "fired" from being party activists.

Then one night at a political reception I talked with the head of an industrial union whom I knew casually. His face lit up when I mentioned the idea of running for county chair. "You should do it!" he said excitedly. "I'll help you." With encouragement from him and many others, I launched my bid for county chair in December. One week after I announced I was running, the current chair announced he would not seek reelection. A month later the executive director quit. It seemed almost too easy. But it turned out to be the hardest job I'd ever taken on.

I ended up serving as co-chair with a man I hardly knew (we later jokingly referred to it as a shotgun marriage). We started out in March with

$300 in the bank and a computer in a box. We worked very hard for eight months, raising over $100,000, hiring four staff members, and involving more than 100 people in committee work. Still, in August, our candidate for governor was down in the polls by 32 points. My income from my consulting business and my co-chair's billable hours at his law firm had both plummeted by 50 percent, but we were not deterred. We were on a mission!

In the months before the election I often prefaced a decision with, "I don't know what to do. I've never done this before!" and my co-chair and staff people would look at me and say, "Neither have we." We plunged ahead anyway.

The last few weeks before the election we had dozens of people show up at the election headquarters every day wanting to help. Some brought food. Some brought their kids along. Their motivation was the same as ours: "We want to help elect a Democratic governor who will lead this state in a different direction."

On Election Day we had 1,000 people volunteering, phoning registered Democrats, poll watching, collecting absentee ballots, and driving people to the polls. And we won! Tom Vilsack was elected governor in November 1998 by 8 percentage points—the biggest comeback in the history of Iowa politics. He won the state by 60,000 votes, half of which came from Polk County.

Often accomplishments and important things in life are done by people who have never done them before. Sometimes when you don't know the "right" way to do things, you find an even better way. If you believe strongly enough in your cause and are willing to work hard and ask for help when you need it, you will succeed. And you might just help elect a governor!

MoveOn Tips

- Gain as much campaign experience as possible doing as many different jobs as you can. Work in different campaigns at different levels to learn how they work.

- Get elected to the county central committee, and attend meetings. Get to know the local party leaders, and volunteer for a project or job that interests you.

- The most important skill you can possess to advance as a volunteer political leader is fund-raising. Ability to raise money quickly is highly sought. Find someone who is good at this, and ask that person to teach you.

- Always make good on your word. Your reputation quickly develops as someone who either gets the job done or doesn't. Other volunteers and staff members definitely notice what you do or don't do. Under-promise and over-deliver.

- Spend time listening and watching. Learn which people are good at what they do and which ones are respected. Observe them and learn.

- A little self-promotion is fine, and probably necessary, but don't make a practice of bragging. Let your work and accomplishments speak for you.

- Most importantly, get to know the people in the party or organization. Politics is all about relationships. Strong relationships are the key to raising money, getting support for your candidate, and enlisting help to get things done. Praise good effort lavishly, and say "thanks" frequently. Build a reputation as someone with whom others want to work.

Peggy Huppert is a mother of three and still active in Iowa Democratic politics. She is executive director of the Chrysalis Foundation, a public foundation dedicated to improving the lives of and empowering women and girls in central Iowa.

Hit the Streets for Your Candidate

Anne H. Thomas, 67, Leesburg, Virginia

On a bright morning, November 3, 2000, I got in my car, map and directions in hand, and drove from Virginia to Philadelphia. I knew that my home state was a lost cause for Democrats and that we needed to win Philadelphia big in order to win Pennsylvania. I walked unannounced into the Democratic party headquarters and said I was ready to work. The headquarters was teeming with people—staffers and volunteers like me. Phones were ringing, people were working phone banks, and huge maps of Philadelphia's districts were everywhere.

Within 15 minutes I had been assigned to a team of four with address lists and Gore/Lieberman handouts, and off we went to ring doorbells for Gore. As soon as we completed our list, we went back to headquarters to be assigned to a new team of four, given more addresses, and sent out again.

My fellow volunteers who weren't Philadelphia residents came from many places on the East Coast—"safe" states like Massachusetts, New Jersey, and Maryland. They arrived by car or carpool, bus, and van. They were mostly young, determined, and focused. The only chatting was in the car, but once we hit the sidewalks we were focused only on working. I had asked them all what motivated them, and their answers were the same as mine: they knew that Bush and the right wing were disastrous for the country, and they felt they had to act.

Throughout the day, citizens opened their doors to me, and we talked. We were in mostly African-American neighborhoods, and I heard over and over that the people living there do not trust Republicans. They told me how trickle-down economics doesn't work and about their desperate need for health care and education. Several of the women hugged me and thanked me for working for Gore.

On Election Day, November 7, our assignment was to hang "door knockers"—small narrow flyers urging residents to vote—on the doorknobs of registered Democrats in a blue-collar neighborhood. When I reported back to headquarters at lunchtime, I began to hear the whispered word "Florida." Lots of cell phones were going, and campaign workers were huddled. Something bad was going on—we knew we probably had to take Florida to win, and even by noon that day stories were circulating about punch cards and citizens prohibited from voting.

We now know the ending to the election story. I think often of all those men and women who hoofed the sidewalks of Philadelphia with me. I never learned their names or who they were, but I know they are waiting to do it again in 2004. I hope you'll come join us.

MoveOn Tips

- Wear clear identification so voters will know who you are.
- Introduce yourself as a volunteer. Voters are much more responsive to volunteers.
- Take every opportunity to talk about your candidate and issues to everyone you encounter as you walk, including people on the street and in stores.
- Have a few concise talking points.
- Instead of trying to convince people who are negative or disinterested, move on to other prospects.
- Handwrite a "Sorry I missed you" card when you have to leave literature (you can write this ahead of time).
- Carry a water bottle and aspirin. Wear comfortable shoes!

Anne H. Thomas is retired from university administration and is currently vice president for political affairs at the Women's National Democratic Club in Washington, DC.

Run for Office to Challenge Incumbents
Michael Fjetland, 54, Sugar Land, Texas

For years I kept a journal as I traveled around the world. I saw things up close that most Americans, even some American leaders, were unaware of. I was in Nicaragua shortly before the Contra War. I got kicked out of the Nile Hilton in Egypt so that the hotel could make room for the signers of the first peace treaty between Israel and an Arab country, negotiated by President Jimmy Carter. In 1990, I was unemployed and writing a book about a fictitious Iraq war and a terrorist attack against the United States. In the middle of my time there Saddam Hussein invaded Kuwait, and I ended up on Fox TV in Houston. Reading my journal made me realize that, even though I'd spent most of my time trying to earn a living, I'd had a recurring interest in politics and improving the world.

As fate would have it, I live in Republican Tom DeLay's district, and I was frustrated with what he was not doing to improve the district and not doing to respond effectively to the rising tide of terrorism worldwide.

Since nothing was getting his attention, in January 2000 I filed to be the first person in years to oppose DeLay in the GOP primary. I didn't have much money, but, because turnout is usually quite small in the primaries and the Democrats didn't have a contested primary in our district that year, I thought it would be possible to pull an upset if enough Democrats crossed over to vote in the GOP primary (this kind of crossover voting is permitted in Texas).

Suddenly, Tom DeLay started appearing at events in the district that he'd missed for years. He'd even skipped the annual Lincoln Day dinner and local chamber of commerce lunches until I came along (not that he follows Lincoln much). To my surprise, DeLay even showed up personally for the ballot draw—in Fort Bend, candidates draw cards for their positions on the ballot—high card gets first position, second highest card gets second position, and so on. At the first draw in Fort Bend, DeLay drew a king. I reached down and drew the ace of spades! Beginner's luck.

I had ten 8-by-10-foot road signs made—the most I could afford.

Suddenly they started disappearing. I caught some guys in a pickup eye-balling one, and when I rolled down my window and said someone had been stealing my signs they took off. When I called in the license plate number, it was a phony.

To my surprise, at a GOP women's club, DeLay himself showed up to debate. Afterward, another GOP candidate came up to me and said that I had won that debate.

Of course I lost the election, but I still won 25 percent of the GOP vote without spending hardly any money on my two-month campaign. The best part is that it forced DeLay to get involved in his district and address some issues that he never would have mentioned if I had been running as a Democrat in a heavily Republican district. Although I didn't win the election, the beneficial results were worth the effort. Now, Tom DeLay is interested in international affairs, and he is finally traveling overseas.

MoveOn Tips

- Concentrate on grassroots approaches. When you're a challenger, no one knows you. Spending on ads is less effective than knocking on people's doors so they see your face. Few will have ever met a candidate, and all appreciate it.

- Get as much free publicity as possible, as opposed to paid ads.

- Keep running and building relationships. Reach out to new voters, and get as many supporters as possible. It takes more than one race to win against an incumbent.

Michael Fjetland is an international attorney, a speaker, and an adjunct professor who is writing a book on the future of America.

Donate Money

Annalise Blum, 16, Berkeley, California

My mom is very politically active and although I try to fight against becoming like her, I realize that it is inevitable—and maybe not such a bad thing. I find myself trying to convince my basketball coach of the existence of global warming. When my history teacher mentioned Barbara Lee in class, I was proud that I had been part of the "Barbara Lee speaks for me" rally.

Even though I cannot vote yet, I have a growing interest in politics. I know that what President Bush is doing will greatly affect the condition of our planet for the rest of my life—and I'm convinced that he must not get elected for a second term. So I was excited when my mom invited me to help pass out information about Wesley Clark at "Unraveling the Lying Liars of the Bush Dynasty"—a panel consisting of Paul Krugman, Al Franken, and Kevin Phillips at the local community theatre. I had read articles about Clark that convinced me his combination of great values and leadership experience made him the best candidate to beat Bush. It was the weekend before finals, and I was quite willing to take a break from studying the Compromise of 1850.

When we first arrived, we walked along the snake-like line, but our offers of Clark literature were met with abrupt responses: "No thanks, I'm for Dean." A few people grudgingly accepted our flyers, but mostly I felt like a fly that people were too polite to shoo away. I left my mom to go get us seats in the theatre. Overhearing the woman next to me discussing the pros and cons of Clark, I offered her more information about him. She initially refused, but a few minutes later decided to take a flyer with McGovern's speech endorsing Clark and read it with interest. When my mom arrived, I excitedly told her about my first success in pamphleteering, and she shared with me her discovery that the line outside the women's bathroom is an excellent place to hand out flyers and talk with people.

At the end of the program, we sprinted toward the doors leading out of the theatre, our Clark flyers in hand. Clark had been mentioned favorably by two of the speakers, and the audience had been energized by the hopeful and humorous political discussions. We smiled broadly at each person exiting as we asked, "Are you interested in Clark information?"

"Sure!" "Yes, I'd like one." "Definitely!"

We gave out more than 300 flyers. It was amazing how much of a difference I felt that I had made. It was a crucial time for Clark in the beginning of the primary season: he had to do well in New Hampshire and he needed more money.

The next day I told my mom: "I've decided to donate $100 to Clark's campaign." I wasn't even thinking about the fact that $100 was two months' allowance or 15 hours of baby-sitting or an entire new outfit from Urban Outfitters. Before my success at passing out flyers, I felt like any contribution I could give would be insignificant—but now I knew that my actions did matter. I have often heard people say that one person can make a difference, but I didn't grasp its truth until I experienced it for myself. When I next wore my jacket, I proudly kept my Clark for President sticker on. Although I won't be able to vote for another two years, politics affects my life, my school, and my world. And hey, if Clark wins, I'm going to tell people that I contributed to his success!

MoveOn Tips

- Don't belittle your ability to contribute. In 2002 the MoveOn Political Action Committee (PAC) raised more than $4 million. The average contribution was $36. Citizens working together are finding that they are a powerful counterweight to special interest groups.

Annalise Blum is a junior in high school in Oakland, California, where she plays basketball and soccer, runs cross country, and volunteers in the community service program.

Host a House Party

Betty Buller Whitehead, 52, Chapel Hill, North Carolina

I was working with other campaign volunteers to plan the first fund-raising party in our area for our presidential candidate. We were seeking a public location for the event, until we discovered that holding the fundraiser in a public place couldn't be approved by the campaign. Due to budget limitations and campaign finance laws, the only way to make our fund-raising party happen was to find a house.

To meet our fund-raising goal, we needed a home that could handle a party of 75 people. We were a fledgling, grassroots group of folks who had come together through Meetup, a free Internet service that organizes local gatherings among people of like interests. I didn't yet know these people, and they didn't know me—but my enthusiasm for my candidate compelled me to take the leap and volunteer my home.

Our house party planning committee transformed into an action group. One man took the lead in organizing the details of the party, including food, beverages, speakers, entertainment, ticket sales and registration, and parking. He also served as the liaison with campaign headquarters. We used the Internet for invitations and responses, eliminating the cost of printing and mailing. The night of the party, a horde of volunteers appeared with food to prepare and put out. They set up tables for registration, arranged chairs so that people could listen to the band we'd hired for entertainment, and provided shuttle service to overcome the limited parking on our dead-end street.

The party was a huge success! In a conference call with other house parties across the country, we got to speak to our candidate. In our house, speakers included a state representative, a local peace activist, and a member of our organizing group. We came together as a community, we were energized by the experience, and we exceeded our fund-raising goal.

MoveOn Tips

- Get fund-raising rules from your candidate's campaign, and keep in touch with campaign staff to ensure compliance as party planning progresses.

- Stretch when setting your goal for numbers of guests and donations.

- Mobilize a small group of committed volunteers to plan everything from invitations to thank-you notes.

- Before guests arrive, plan where and when each activity of the party will take place.

- Assign responsibility to specific people for everything from name tags to pouring drinks.

- Make it a party. Have fun!

Betty Buller Whitehead is a retired hospital administrator, currently pursuing a part-time career in acting and writing. She lives with her husband, two sons, two cats, and a dog.

Petition Effectively

Ruth Hultgren, 82, Sacramento, California

Many petition circulators these days are mercenaries, paid for each signature they get. However, a substantial coterie of us still are volunteers dedicated to the cause for which we are petitioning. We actually have a few things to learn from the mercenaries. My chapter of Peace Action hired a professional petitioning company to train us. They taught us the best words to use to stop a passerby and, indeed, the best way to dismiss a heckler.

In the past, I'd sometimes found it difficult to be sufficiently assertive to gain the attention of people passing my petition table in a mall. I used to feel apologetic about stopping busy shoppers. But since the training, forget a table! I now use an ironing board. People stop out of curiosity, coming close enough to glance at my clipboards and to hear my opener, "I have a petition for you." Not a question—a statement, which almost requires the person to ask, "About what?" (I do not say, "Would you like to sign a petition?" or "Have you seen this petition?" These openers can easily elicit "No" as the person moves out of range.)

Quickly I continue, "Hundreds have signed this petition to Senator Feinstein to ask for an independent commission to investigate apparent lies about Iraq having 'weapons of mass destruction.' Please join us in pressing her to get the truth. Sign here." I then extend a pen to my visitor, angled to write. I offer to hold the baby or watch a toddler while young parents write their names and addresses. I even hold packages for the signature writer.

If my visitors have extensive doubts or questions, I am ready with a succinct clipping or informational flyer that explains the issue. I'll respond to their first question; by their third question, even if it's not hostile, I know this person is wasting my time. If someone persists in the discussion, which is generally a sign of a heckler, I always say, "Well, it looks like we have a lot of educational work to do on this matter. Could you put $20 in our donation box here to help out?" I have never known a heckler who did anything but walk away in a huff, thus relieving me to continue my other contacts.

My signature production grew 500 percent under this tutelage, and I have twice been in campaigns that collected 12,000 citizens' signatures by these almost painless methods. Petitioning face-to-face is an empowering experience for me. I meet my fellow Americans, who are also concerned and willing to speak out for change. Those who disagree with me only inspire me to work harder. After all, it's my great-grandchildren's future at stake.

MoveOn Tips

- Open with the statement "I have a petition for you," instead of a question.
- Make sure that any clipboard top page already has several signatures, and include a sheaf of previously signed petitions under the first page. People will sign if they feel they are not alone.
- When people sign, don't bombard them with flyers unless they request a supply.
- Don't embellish your ironing board with stacks of informational flyers, which can be intimidating or off-putting. Instead, relate to people as a straightforward, helpful fellow citizen.
- Don't waste time trying to convince people who want to monopolize your time. Just move on to reach the person who sympathizes with your cause.

Ruth Hultgren is an activist great-grandmother, was a founding board member in 1984 of Sacramento Area Peace Action, and is a retired preschool teacher. She and her husband, Wayne, have recruited and trained many petitioners.

Attend a Meetup

Bob Rouillard, 32, Rochester, Minnesota

In early April, I heard a speech rebroadcast on C-SPAN by Democratic presidential candidate Howard Dean. In it he challenged Democrats about not standing up against George W. Bush's reckless policies. I was so impressed that I called his campaign headquarters to see how I could get involved with the campaign where I live. The woman who took my call said there was no Minnesota office, but she suggested I sign up for a Meetup with other Dean supporters.

Soon after I signed up, I got an email from Meetup about a forthcoming gathering, but I almost didn't go. I'd never really been involved in politics. I didn't know who any of these people were. Then my wife said, "Just go," shooing me out the door.

So I went to the Meetup for Dean, and found four highly intelligent people: a union organizer, a software engineer, a minister, and a college professor. Although we had very different backgrounds, we all felt we had to do something to take the country back from moneyed interests.

We planned a house party fund-raiser at my house for the following month. I didn't know what that meant, but I figured "what the heck!" I called the Dean campaign, and the people there told me the rules about money they could and couldn't accept. I was going to make a difference! We were going to take our country back!

For the first time in my life I felt optimistic about politics. I realized that politics could work if only more people like me would get involved. I was sure that there were more like me. Our next Meetup had 15 people; the next, 25; the next, 40. Sure enough, there were more people like me. I couldn't believe I'd never done this before. I felt it was what I was made to do.

Since then, I've tabled, signed petitions, voted in the MoveOn primary, and gone door-to-door. Hundreds of people have gotten involved in politics in my little corner of the world because of the work I've done. As a result of the optimism I feel every day, I will always stay politically active. I'm hooked!

MoveOn Tips

- Try attending a Meetup gathering. Meetup (www.meetup. com) is a free service that enables people to organize local gatherings. The meetings are casual get-togethers where peers talk. Attendees vote on where Meetups will happen, so you may end up at a bar, a local café, or a bowling alley. Sometimes simultaneous Meetups take place in cities all over the world. Many candidates have been using this service to support their campaigns.

- If you host a Meetup, arrive early, bring a sign so that others can find you, and try to introduce everyone to one another.

Bob Rouillard works at the Mayo Clinic and is the father of Lillian, nine, and Rowan, seven. In the past he's voted Green, Reform, Natural Law, Democratic, and Republican, but George W. Bush has forced him to concentrate his efforts and call himself a Democrat.

Serve as an Elected Official

Hannah Pingree, 27, North Haven, Maine

E very action we take can move us toward progress—whether it is donating our money and time or lobbying a politician. Yet the one form of leadership those of us who want to change the world often overlook is running for office. If we are committed to making a difference, what better role to take on than that of decision maker?

I grew up on an island 12 miles off the coast of Maine. It is a place where everyone knows everyone. In March our entire town packs into the community gymnasium for our annual town meeting, where we vote on the town budget items, elect local officers, and discuss local policies. Most islanders attend town meeting every year and understand that their voices and votes play a major role in helping our small community survive.

In my town of just 350 people, there are 90 elected and appointed officials, from the school board to the recreation council. For me, growing up in a small place where virtually everyone must participate, it never occurred to me that being involved was an option rather than a necessity.

That being said, making the decision to run for office is not easy for anyone. There are always so many reasons not to run, and the excuses are endless. I was 25 when I decided to run for the state legislature, and I wasn't sure I was ready. I felt too young and inexperienced. But after seeking advice from local leaders, family, and neighbors, I decided to run anyway.

In Maine we have publicly financed races and small campaign budgets, so to win you must get out and meet as many voters as possible. Most of this happens by knocking on doors. I ran to represent a district that included 11 towns, 9 of which were islands.

Knocking on the door of a person you don't know is a sometimes strange and sometimes wonderful experience. I met elderly citizens who loved having my company, bare-chested fishermen with articulate concerns, and working moms who wanted to talk politics while they cooked dinner. After more than a thousand doors, many conversations, mailings, and phone calls, one church basement debate, and countless cups of coffee, I won a seat in my state legislature.

To serve in a state legislature is just as dynamic and challenging as running. My peers are teachers and farmers, lawyers and doctors, single parents and retired people. Some days we debate issues that seem very far afield from my island communities, and other days I get to fight for things that will have a direct impact on the people I represent. Even as a freshman lawmaker, I have seen from inside the process that so much is possible. I have watched bills and budgets change for the better when one legislator raises a valid concern or when the public comes in large numbers to a public hearing. We really do have the ability to affect the process in a positive way. Government and politicians can best deliver the kind of change we want when *we* are the government and politicians.

MoveOn Tips

- When campaigning for office, always ask people what they think first. People like (and need) to be heard, and representing their needs will be your job.

- Be honest. People appreciate that more than anything, even if you don't agree.

- Don't be afraid to ask people to help you in your campaign— you're giving them the opportunity to get involved.

- Focus on two or three really important ideas that you know will change your community and affect people's lives.

Hannah Pingree is currently the youngest woman in the Maine house of representatives, representing the islands and coastal towns of District 129.

Act Outside the Box

Diane MacEachern, 51, Takoma Park, Maryland

When you work on the same issue day in and day out, month after month, year after year, it's pretty easy to get burned out, no matter how important the issue is or how strongly you feel about it.

This was the situation "bottle bill" activists faced in the late 1970s. Citizens in dozens of states had been organizing for years to try to pass legislation that would require consumers to pay a five- or ten-cent deposit on soft drink and beer cans and bottles to ensure that they would be returned to stores rather than end up as litter on the street. Similar laws that had been passed in Oregon, Vermont, Michigan, and Maine were shown to reduce litter and solid waste substantially, as well as save energy and promote recycling. Many grassroots groups were trying to pass bottle bills in their own states and give momentum to national deposit legislation.

But the challenge was tough. The soda and beer industries strenuously opposed bottle bills and spent millions of dollars defeating every grassroots campaign that was launched. After several years, citizens groups were discouraged; it looked like another bottle bill would never become law.

In 1977, I went to work at Environmental Action in Washington, DC, to help activists bolster their bottle bill campaigns. As I talked with organizers and volunteers around the country, it became clear that, while people were committed to the issue, they were tired of fighting an enemy who had a lot more power and resources than they did. They needed an organizing tactic that would help unify their efforts, generate some much-needed local media exposure, spark interest nationally—and revive the spirits of their volunteers.

As I looked at the ubiquitous throwaway beverage container that was causing all the trouble, an idea hit me. Why not get activists from all over the country to mail thousands of empty soda and beer cans to the White House? With one simple action, we could pressure President Carter to support a national bottle bill, create a local publicity event, and have some fun!

I quickly designed a sticky, can-sized label that read: "Dear President

Carter: This beverage container is only 1 of 70 billion that contribute to the trashing of America annually. Throwaways also represent wasted energy. A national deposit law could save 81,000 barrels of oil per day. As an alternative to waste, I support a national deposit on all beer and soft drink bottles and cans. President Carter, please urge Congress to adopt deposit legislation." A blank line allowed the sender to sign his or her name.

Thousands of labels were sent to local organizers, along with ideas on how to collect cans and hold media events. As long as the cans carried the proper amount of postage, and the lids were sealed so that they wouldn't injure postal workers, they could be legally mailed. Hundreds of organizers had mailing parties at which they were able to recruit new volunteers for their campaigns. They held press conferences at local post offices when they mailed their cans to the White House, and they even got local schools, churches, and civic groups involved in the effort. Meanwhile, I mailed cans labeled with press releases to reporters and editors at newspapers, radio stations, and television stations. Though the media had dismissed bottle bills as "old" news, they found it pretty hard to ignore a press release wrapped around a can.

All in all, the response to the "Cans to Carter" campaign far surpassed my expectations. During the course of the effort, President Carter received over 50,000 cans from concerned citizens all across the United States. Each time the president received another 10,000 cans, we put out another news release. By the end of the campaign, we had generated a whopping 1,300 newspaper, radio, and television news stories.

Once we passed the 50,000 cans mark, we convinced the U.S. Senate to hold hearings on whether the United States should have a national bottle bill. That was not a victory we were able to secure, but our efforts helped inspire activists working to pass bottle bills in many states. Eventually Connecticut, Delaware, Hawai'i, Iowa, Massachusetts, and New York passed their own bills. By 2002, 11 states had container deposit laws.

MoveOn Tips

- Do something unique that relates specifically to your campaign. The more unusual and creative you can get, the more volunteers and activists you'll recruit to your effort, the more money you'll raise to support it—and the more fun you'll have.

- Make your activity as easy and straightforward as possible. Provide clear directions, a specific timeframe, and solid benchmarks, so those participating can achieve small gains en route to their bigger victory.

- Leave room for creativity on the part of those who get involved in the project. Once you give them an idea, get out of their way and let them run with it.

- Always include "Alert the media" in your action plans. And remember: The more unusual and creative you get, the more media attention you'll receive.

Diane MacEachern is an author and activist who lives with her husband and two teenagers.

V: Personal Action Is Political

Introduction

Gail Sheehy, Author and Journalist

I was afraid the post-Boomers were so turned off by our bought political bloviators that they would retreat permanently into cynical couch potato-ism. But idealism lives! MoveOn is initiating the apolitical generations into progressive political action—and just in time. The brilliance of MoveOn's founders is that they're doing politics your way. Online, interactively, inclusively. You can be part of the action and still be a couch potato.

The halls of Congress are crawling with shiny-shoed lobbyists and big-spending defense contractors who can help make or break a politician's chances for reelection. Our elected representatives court reelection by pleasing these power brokers. The tropism among both groups is to exist only for themselves. Some call it Versailles on the Potomac—a hall of mirrors.

Who can shatter this static image? You can. How? There are four words that get any politician's attention when voiced passionately by a constituent group: We're not going away. I offer you the example of four moms from New Jersey, who are among the stars of my book, *Middletown, America,* which chronicles the aftermath of 9/11.

"Okay, there's the House and the Senate—which one has the most members?" Lorie Van Aucken laughed at herself. "I must have slept through that civics class." It was April 2002, seven months after Lorie had lost her husband Kenneth in the terrorist attacks on the World Trade Center. She and three other young 9/11 widows were planning a political rally on Capitol Hill to demand an independent investigation of the failures to prevent and respond to the attacks. They had all thought themselves exempt from politics, by virtue of the constant emergency of motherhood.

Kristen Breitweiser, although she was only 30, was somewhat better informed than the other three widows. She had graduated from law school, practiced all of three days, hated it, and elected to be a full-time mom. Her first line of defense against despair was to revert to thinking like a lawyer, posing questions to journalists like me: "How could there be such a colossal, systemic, utter failure that morning? Between the FAA, the NSA

[National Security Agency], the CIA, the Secret Service, the FBI? There is no possible way that four planes could be simultaneously hijacked above the United States and no one know how to stop them until they hit their targets. We spend billions of dollars on national defense for intelligence. I don't understand why normal American citizens don't find this mildly disturbing."

The four moms began surfing the net, collecting their own information, and building a network of netwarriors. They made weekly trips to Washington in Kristen's SUV to do "widow walkabouts" and persuade legislators to support the idea of an independent commission. On the day of their big rally in DC, only a few of the big guns showed up. The four moms began speaking passionately to a crowd of about 100 of the 10,000 family members robbed of loved ones by 9/11: "Why, hours after the first hijacked plane crashed into the Trade Center, was it up to Todd Beamer and other brave passengers to keep Flight 93 from crashing into this building behind us?" Word spread on the Hill that the rally was getting wall-to-wall coverage by the media. Chairs on the platform began filling with an impressive lineup of senators and representatives, Democratic and Republican, all of whom saw a chance to be on the right side of a noble cause.

Three months later, Kristen was delegated by the family groups to testify on their behalf in the first public hearings before the House-Senate Joint Inquiry on Intelligence. A spokesperson for the CIA had ridiculed her appearance in advance in print: "Do we really need weeping widows? Is this going to be an Oprah moment?"

Unfazed, the young widow took her seat at the long witness table. She looked up at the raised firmament of House and Senate committee members and their batteries of staffers. Kristen sat alone. Lorie slipped her a box of Dots candies, to remind her she was there to connect the dots. It made Kristen chuckle. And then she gave 20 minutes of staggeringly concrete evidence of the failures of the country's leadership, past and present, to execute its most fundamental responsibility—to protect its citizens against foreign attack.

The measure of Kristen's success was an invitation to the White House the next day. The president's political advisers, who had been doing everything in their power to block an independent commission, reversed course. The day after, the Senate approved a broad independent inquiry by an overwhelming vote, 90 to 8. This triumph was followed by a bait-and-switch game by the Bush Administration, appearing to be supportive while raising every conceivable obstacle to thwart the idea. But the four moms have kept the momentum of their cause alive by impressing the same four words on everyone they lobby: "We're not going away."

The 9/11 Commission wouldn't have happened without the four moms, says former congressman Tim Roemer, who coauthored the enabling legislation. He congratulated them, "At a time when many Americans don't even take the opportunity to cast a ballot, you folks went out and made the legislative system work."

Jamie Gorelick, a highly respected former deputy U.S. attorney general, addressed the four moms at a televised hearing: "I'm enormously impressed that laypeople with no powers of subpoena, with no access to insider information of any sort, could put together a very powerful set of questions and set of facts that are a road map for this commission. It is really quite striking. Now, what's your secret?" Mindy Kleinberg, who had given blistering testimony at that day's hearing, said simply, "Eighteen months of doing nothing but grieving and connecting the dots."

If four moms with broken hearts and home lives shattered by terrorism can make their voices heard at the top echelons of their government, so can you. The following chapter suggests many ways you can get a move on.

Serve Your Community

Arthur I. Blaustein, 67, Berkeley, California

My first experience as a volunteer was in 1964. While I was a graduate student at Columbia, I worked for the Congress of Racial Equality (CORE) doing research on conditions at a migrant labor camp. That experience taught me invaluable lessons I've taken with me through the years. And I'm still learning from community service today, in my role as a volunteer faculty adviser to the AmeriCorps program on the University of California, Berkeley, campus.

After 30 years of firsthand experience as a volunteer, and after working with hundreds of volunteers, I can say with certainty that community service is very much a two-way street. It is about giving and receiving. The very act of serving taps into a wellspring of empathy and generosity that is both personally gratifying and energizing.

I saw this in action five years ago, when I decided to give the students in my American studies classes, mostly university seniors, the choice between a midsemester exam or 16 hours of community service. The students unanimously chose service, though most of them didn't know what was in store for them. They had a choice of about 60 activities, which were organized by the Public Service Center at the university.

Here's what one student wrote about this experience: "Last week, I learned that one of my favorite children is homeless. It seems so silly to be reprimanding him for not doing his homework and not putting in the effort at school. This seems so trivial compared to the real-life horrors that he must experience. I find myself yearning to become a teacher, which was a career I never thought about before this program. I know that as these children grow, they will probably forget about me; but I know I will never forget them. I have truly changed and matured as a result of them."

This type of comment is typical of what I hear from my students. More formal academic research and evaluations show that "service-learning" (the combination of volunteerism and related academic studies) clearly enriches and enhances the individual volunteer in multiple ways.

My students experience the same kinds of internal transformations that I did 37 years ago, when I taught in Harlem during the early years of the War on Poverty and Volunteers in Service to America (VISTA)—now part of AmeriCorps. When we volunteer, we are confronted with the complexities of the everyday worlds of individuals we might never otherwise connect with, as well as communities quite different from our own. We are forced to deal with difficult social and economic realities. It was a revelation to learn about the inequities and injustices of our society, to see firsthand the painful struggles of children who did not have the educational, social, or economic opportunities that many of us take for granted.

Ethical values and healthy communities are not inherited; either they are re-created through action by each generation, or they are not. Creating those values and communities is what makes AmeriCorps, VISTA, and other forms of community service unique and valuable. They help us to regenerate our best values and principles as individuals and as a society.

The goals of service are inclusive and nourishing: to honor diversity, protect the environment, and enrich our nation's educational, social, and economic policies so that they enhance human dignity. On a personal level, volunteering—the very act of caring and doing—makes a substantial difference in our individual lives because it nourishes the moral intelligence required for critical judgment and mature behavior.

Community service helps us integrate our idealism and realism. An idealist without a healthy dose of realism tends to become a naïve romantic. A realist without ideals tends to become a cynic. Service helps us put our ideals to work in a realistic setting.

At her memorial service, it was said of Eleanor Roosevelt, the most influential American woman of the 20th century, that "she would rather light a candle than curse the darkness." What was true for her then is true for us now. The choice to make a difference is ours.

MoveOn Tips

- Choose your volunteer activity to suit your individual passions, talents, and interests. For example, consider whether you'd prefer to work directly with those you're helping or more behind the scenes. The more you care, the more likely you'll be to stick with it.

- Most volunteer opportunities offer a range of time commitments. Make a commitment to an organization and to yourself to volunteer a certain amount of time each week or month. Even a few hours a month can make a difference.

- Enlist your family, friends, co-workers, or organization in the activity. Volunteering together strengthens ties, and it's great for children.

- Use VolunteerMatch, a nonprofit, online service that helps interested volunteers get involved with community service organizations throughout the United States. Enter your zip code on the VolunteerMatch website (www.volunteer-match.org) to find local volunteer opportunities.

- Check out the Corporation for National and Community Service, in service to help strengthen communities (www.cns.gov/).

- Apply to AmeriCorps, a network of national service programs that engage more than 50,000 Americans each year in intensive service to meet critical needs in education, public safety, health, and the environment (www.americorps.org/).

- If you're 25 or younger, try SERVEnet (www.servenet.org/), which matches young volunteers with organizations. SERVEnet is a program of Youth Service America (YSA) (www.ysa.org/), a resource center that partners with organizations committed to increasing the quality and quantity of opportunities for young Americans, ages 5 to 25, to volunteer.

Arthur I. Blaustein is a professor at the University of California, Berkeley, where he teaches community development, urban policy, and social history. His most recent books are *Make a Difference: America's Guide to Volunteering* and *The American Promise: Justice and Opportunity.*

Defy City Hall

Jerilyn Fay Kelle, 53, Richmond, Virginia

In 1979, I was living in rural Kay County, Oklahoma. I'd never done anything remotely political when an accident changed my life. The teenage son of a farmer crashed the family grain truck while hauling the farm's load of grain to the local co-op. At the time, I worked for an insurance agent and always carried a camera, so I took pictures and talked to the family members. They explained that the boy had never driven a fully loaded truck, so when he had to dodge a huge pothole in the county road, the truck overturned, breaking the axle. The small family farmer had postponed buying auto insurance until he got the proceeds from the harvest. With no insurance, the family lost the truck and shortly thereafter the farm.

I was heartbroken for them. It was then that I started noticing that the roads where smaller farmers lived had more potholes than where bigger, better-off farmers lived. Even though I had been raised in a working-poor family of nine children, I no longer lived "on the poor side of town." When I started asking questions, people close to me told me not to worry about it, since my roads were in good shape. But I couldn't forget about it after seeing the defeat and hopelessness in that farmer's eyes.

My questions eventually led me to my own county commissioner's office. I was petrified. I had never approached a public official before in my life. I was carrying my young son as I approached his desk. When I tentatively asked him about the bad roads and showed him my pictures, I'm sure my hands and voice were shaking. He leaned back in his chair, slammed his boots on his desk, and told me to take my boy and go back to the kitchen where I belonged. Pointing to the front door, he said, "You'll be better off if you leave me alone and let me do my job."

Ironically, if he had tried to reassure or appease me, I might have dropped the issue. Instead, infuriated, I wrote letters to several local newspapers. To my surprise, my letter explaining what had happened and my pictures of the potholes were published. Sometime later, the Oklahoma Bureau of Investigation assigned undercover agents to shadow our commissioners, and the agents documented that the money allocated for road repair was instead going into the commissioners' pockets. By the end of 1981, almost every county commissioner in the state had been arrested and indicted for corruption.

I can't take credit for the investigation or the outcome, but I'm proud that I didn't just walk away, allowing that poor excuse for a public servant to silence me. I didn't know that the commissioners were swindling hard-working Oklahoma citizens, but his not listening (in fact, insulting me) was a sign that something was very wrong. This was not the America I had learned to be proud of. This was not self-government in action. When I saw that he was neglecting those ideals, I didn't give up on them—I became more determined to make him, my government official, live up to them.

Reinforced with a renewed belief in what citizens can and must do to hold onto their democratic way of life, I later competed for and won a national women's fellowship to work on Capitol Hill. After that, I became a lobbyist and grassroots organizer.

My journey began in a tiny town because a county commissioner refused to listen to me. I got from there to here solely because I never lost faith in the American ideals of liberty and justice for all, and especially because I never surrendered my steadfast conviction in the word "all."

MoveOn Tips

- Approach your public official with the intention of creating a dialogue, allowing both of you to express your views and concerns.

- Enter into the discussion with a calm and reasonable attitude. Emotions will naturally infuse your speech, but don't set the tone to be a heated debate.

- Prepare for your meeting by gathering evidence that supports your concern—news clippings, photos, and personal testimonies. Realize that the official simply may not be aware of the issue.

Jerilyn Fay Kelle, Ph.D., is an assistant professor at Mary Baldwin College.

Respond Locally to National Issues

Brenda Koehler, 51, Mohnton, Pennsylvania

My friend Charyn sent out an email seeking support for a resolution opposing enforcement of the Patriot Act in our town. The Patriot Act was passed in October 2001 purportedly to apprehend terrorists, but it actually deprives American citizens of essential rights. It permits the government to deny U.S. citizens the right to an attorney; search our houses without warrants; imprison us secretly; hold us indefinitely without charges; search our email; view our medical, financial, and educational records; and wiretap our conversations without a court order—among other things. I went to the city council meeting not because I thought the resolution would pass but because I felt the need to take a principled stand. In those dark days after the preemptive bombing of Iraq, I wanted to be a part of something idealistic and democratic, even if it was only a token effort.

Supporters of the petition overflowed the city council chambers and spilled out into the hall. This unexpected showing blindsided the council's tacit decision to dismiss the petition without even reading the 300-page Patriot Act. The councilmembers had assumed that the act's reassuring title was reflective of its content, but in the face of so many potential opponents, they postponed the hearing for a week to give themselves a chance to actually read the document.

At the hearing a week later on April 28, the council chambers were packed with people whose fundamental regard for autonomy and self-determination had prevailed over their striking differences. There were tattooed white-power supporters, T-shirted members of the Green party, impeccably dressed attorneys and academics, prosperous-looking business owners, and Democrats in long flowing skirts—a diverse group whose combined numbers constituted an imposing and powerful force.

The first and most compelling speaker from the crowd was Roy Frankhouser, former Grand Dragon of the Ku Klux Klan and notorious white supremacist. Frankhouser gave a passionate, thundering speech on individual freedoms that was met with wild applause despite his dubious ideology. I sat on the sidelines, stunned by his mastery, alternately thinking, "This is wonderful!" "No, it's terrible!"

Dr. Fred Rich, a distinguished, white-haired Quaker, quoted Benjamin Franklin, who said, "Those who would sell their freedoms for a little security deserve neither."

Dr. Nancy Omaha Boy, an associate dean at Rutgers University, informed the audience that the county's representative in the House, Tim Holden, had voted on the Patriot Act without even knowing what it contained, because it had been forced through Congress so quickly.

Attorney Susan Scholl presented several examples of how the Patriot Act had already infringed on citizens' freedoms in the past year. One was the arrest and five-hour questioning of attorney Andrew O'Connor for typing the words "Bush is out of control" on a library computer.

There were many more inspiring speeches that night, from Stefan Kosikowski, the Green party chair; Dawn Williams, a young community college student; and Jennaro Pullano, another member of the Green party. After every speech the chamber resounded with loud, prolonged, and emphatic applause.

Because our town is such a model of tradition and straitlaced conservatism, many of the people in attendance (including myself) did not think a resolution to refuse to enforce the Patriot Act would pass. At the end of the night, the council's vote to refuse to enforce it by a majority of five to two was an exhilarating victory. As I walked home, the distinctly American realization of having leveraged a change in my own community was intoxicating.

MoveOn Tips

- To implement a resolution to oppose enforcing the Patriot Act in your own town, go to www.bordc.org/Tools.htm for information and support.

Brenda Koehler is a nontraditional student attending college in Kutztown, Pennsylvania. She's a former mail carrier turned writing student.

Attend a Rally

Micheline Aharonian Marcom, 35, Berkeley, California

I am a fiction writer, and for the past six years I have been working on a trilogy that focuses on the genocide of Armenians in Ottoman Turkey during the First World War and its aftermath. I believe that fiction can and does make an important contribution to political awareness, but I also know that sometimes action is called for. Then artists must leave their ateliers and, like other humanist and antiwar compatriots, put their bodies on the street to address the injustices of the day in the moment.

In the winter and spring of 2003, I, like millions of people around the world, took to the streets to protest a war that had not yet begun. The turnout broke all records. The unprecedented numbers in an unprecedented situation—demonstrating against a proposed war—was an inspiration and a fount of hope.

Prior to the demonstration of February 15, 2003, I'd been depressed and worried beyond belief about what the radical conservatives in the White House were doing and how they were taking all of us, American and non-American alike, down a path that we feared had no return. I felt obligated as a citizen to join with the people of the Bay Area to give a very physical "no" to what our government—because we do have to claim it as ours—was doing.

So, for the first time in many years I took to the streets, this time with my husband and young son. We loaded up the stroller and a heavy order of snacks, jackets, blankets, water bottles, milk bottles, and assorted toys. We arranged to meet our neighbors and closest friends in front of our house. By nine o'clock in the morning we had all assembled, 14 of us, including several babies and pregnant mothers.

It was a beautiful winter day: clear blue skies and a cool sharp wind. As we walked, we began to notice dozens of people heading in the same direction, and the closer we got, the more people we saw. There was exhilaration at that moment: We were not alone, and there were people from every walk of life—small babies in slings and strollers, people holding placards, and all manners of hairstyle and dress. The sounds of conga drums and strumming guitars surrounded us.

It was obvious—given the tenor, the joy actually, of the massed crowd—that we all needed to know, to physically *see*, that so many American citizens were opposed to the bellicose plans of our government. And that so many Americans would, in times of duress, exercise their First Amendment right with exuberance and verve.

I held my son on my shoulders for long periods so that he could get a glimpse of the crowd—a mass of humanity that stretched farther than the human eye could see in either direction along San Francisco's Market Street. I wondered if he would remember this day, but I knew that it didn't matter, that we would tell him about it, instruct him in the importance of civil action and civil service if democracy is to continue to thrive in these United States.

MoveOn Tips

- Exercise your right to free speech today. To get started, visit www.protest.net for events happening in your community.

Micheline Aharonian Marcom's latest novel is *The Daydreaming Boy,* published in April 2004 by Riverhead Books.

Instigate Protective Laws

Rosemary Shahan, 54, Sacramento, California

When I started protesting at a car dealership in Lemon Grove, California, I never dreamed of the impact it would have on my life and on the rights of millions of auto owners around the nation. My car had been in a collision at an intersection that was "blind" and lacked any stop or yield signs. I took the car to the dealership for repairs, and the service staff promised it would be fixed in a couple of weeks. But they kept stalling, saying it would be done "any day." Meanwhile they had it in pieces. After three months, they admitted they had not even ordered all the parts. I started contacting various agencies, seeking help. They were sympathetic but said there was little they could do. Without my car, I found it very hard to get to work, get groceries, or function normally.

Finally, in utter desperation, I started to picket. I ended up picketing for five months, while the dealer stonewalled. At first, I was probably the world's worst picketer. People couldn't read my signs, I got badly sunburned, and my feet hurt. The owner's son tried to have me arrested. I've never been arrested, and the threat was somewhat intimidating. But the police came out and talked with him. Then they talked to me, and they whispered privately, "Don't give up." After that, they would drive by and give me the thumbs-up. I made better signs, wore a big hat to keep off the sun, and got used to being on my feet so much. I picketed evenings and weekends, as many hours as I could, often getting rides from friends, colleagues, and neighbors.

A TV station did a story about my plight, and people starting honking and waving when they drove by. One by one, people stopped and told me their car horror stories, about how they had sunk their savings into absolute nightmare cars. I was struck by the gross injustice of their plights and began to realize that my sour experience was just the tip of the iceberg. Most of all, I was concerned that they were compelled to drive unsafe vehicles. I started to research the laws consumers could use to get relief from sour deals, and I realized that California's warranty law had a fatal flaw. It allowed manufacturers a "reasonable number" of repair attempts before the buyer could get a refund or replacement. But the manufacturers' idea of reasonable was totally *unreasonable*. Eventually, a representative from Ford testified that the company expected to have 30 tries to fix a problem.

I decided we needed a "lemon law" to set a guideline for what is reasonable, so I started handing out flyers asking people to write to the chair of the Assembly Consumer Protection Committee, then Assemblyman Bill Lockyer, in Sacramento, California. Some friends and neighbors told me I was wasting my time. But my family encouraged me, and I kept at it. Consumer advocates with the California Public Interest Research Group (CALPIRG), founded by Ralph Nader, also offered encouragement and suggested creative ways to involve the community.

The notion of a lemon law started to catch on. Lemon owners showed me letters they were getting back from the capitol. Lockyer wrote that his office was getting "a great deal of mail." He scheduled a legislative hearing in San Diego. I rounded up lemon owners, who testified. One of the committee members, Assemblywoman Sally Tanner, introduced a bill. It redefined "reasonable" as 30 days out of service and/or four attempts to repair a major problem.

I organized the people who had stopped by while I was picketing in Lemon Grove, and we held a "lemon-aid parade." We marched, holding up huge, colorful all-day suckers, along with signs saying, If We Stick Together, We Can Lick Them! The parade generated great news coverage.

For months, the dealership employees had been harassing me and fellow picketers, gesturing as if they were shooting us with rifles and threatening to run us over with their vans. The judge issued a restraining order. Finally, the dealership owner agreed to talk. Because I didn't trust the work done at the dealership, I negotiated that the dealer would buy my car and pay $25 per day from the date his staff said it would be ready until the date he finally agreed to settle. I took the winnings and started a new consumer group.

The auto industry fought back tooth and nail. It took three years of organizing, letter-writing campaigns, testifying, press conferences, and keeping up the heat, but in 1982 Governor Jerry Brown signed California's landmark Lemon Law. Eventually, the California law became a model for similar laws enacted in the other 49 states. Minnesota Attorney General

Skip Humphrey, writing on behalf of the attorneys general of all 50 states, said, "State new car lemon laws are the single most important advance in consumer protection in the last decade."

At the time, the auto industry had more influence in Washington, and President Reagan was deregulating protection against unsafe, defective vehicles. But once the states took up the cause, manufacturers had to respond to a groundswell of citizen activism.

During the past 20 years, state lemon laws have forced manufacturers to give refunds to hundreds of thousands of beleaguered lemon owners. Once, when the industry tried to gut California's Lemon Law, we rented a red pickup truck and dumped 800 pounds of lemons at the state capitol. That event generated national news and led the amending bill's author to change the law from one that was harmful to consumers to one that offered further protections. Today, I am still advocating for consumers to get safe, reliable transportation and a fair deal. And I know what a difference a small group of engaged citizens can make.

MoveOn Tips

- Reach out to others in the same boat, and join forces with other groups that share your goals.

- Be prepared for setbacks, and don't let them stop you.

- Find lawmakers who will stand up to powerful special interests on behalf of the public. Then give them recognition, letting voters know that they are on the public's side.

- Involve the news media in covering your cause. Don't get discouraged if they don't cover you at first—keep building your expertise, always tell the truth, and always take time to meet with reporters and editors.

- Remain committed to nonviolent, peaceful means of reaching your goals.

Rosemary Shahan is the president of Consumers for Auto Reliability and Safety.

Initiate a Constitutional Amendment

Alfred Dreyfus Samuelson, 50, Washington, DC

"Drey, you've done less with more talent than anyone I know," my father told me in 1982, after I'd taken a job with the tiny, struggling Nebraska Farmers Union. He wanted me to become a lawyer and perhaps join his practice, but my public-speaking phobia eliminated law school as a possibility, and my 29 years were distinguished only by a lack of achievement. Which seemed somehow fitting, since many saw the Farmers Union as a fading relic of the Populist movement that had failed to live up to its own potential.

However, in 1981, Prudential Insurance Company shocked the state's rural leaders by purchasing 30,000 acres of environmentally sensitive Sandhills land and slapping center-pivot irrigation systems on it. This purchase threatened not only the environment but also, if more purchases followed, the livelihood of Nebraska farmers—who would suffer a huge and unfair competitive disadvantage.

In 1982, the Farmers Union, led by Neil Oxton, decided to initiate a state constitutional amendment that would outlaw further corporate farmland purchases or production of livestock. Most folks told Oxton that his plan was a huge mistake; if he failed to get the necessary signatures, or if the measure lost in the general election, the Nebraska Farmers Union would look foolish, and the cause would be set back for years. But doing nothing was worse, and he made the brave and audacious decision to move forward.

Realizing that he needed help, Oxton hired me to get the required 60,000 signatures. I had five months and a handful of volunteers. After three months of very hard work, we had only 15,000 signatures. We were doomed, and I knew it. My dad was right about me. There was only one glimmer of hope: we'd given out blank petitions to some of the folks who'd signed, when they indicated that they were willing to circulate the petition to others. I sent out a last-ditch letter to those 1,500 people, noting: "Prudential will win unless we act. It's now or never."

By the first part of June—the last of our five months—the trickle of petitions had turned into what felt to me like the "mighty river of justice" in the Book of Amos. Amazingly, every day thousands of signatures arrived in the mail and, in early July, "Initiative 300" was certified for the general election ballot.

In late August, a big-business coalition announced that it would raise and spend $500,000 to defeat our initiative, labeling it "anti–free enterprise." By contrast, our Family Farm Coalition barely had two nickels among us; we would be swamped.

The news media love a good fight, and this one caught their imagination; it became the biggest story in the state. I was soon thrust into a role for which I was completely unprepared: public spokesman. I was terrified.

It wasn't long before the requests for televised debates came in, and Oxton gave me the assignment of defending the initiative. I was too ashamed to admit my fears to him but also scared out of my wits at the prospect of being unable to speak on statewide TV. When the time came, to my utter amazement, I held my own. My confidence soared, and I found myself in the surprising position of actually looking forward to my next TV debate, which I clearly won.

Still, the initiative was hardly home free. Nebraskans were assaulted by anti–Initiative 300 TV and radio ads, direct mail, and editorials. It felt as though the entire Nebraska power structure were against us. The last two polls differed—one showed us winning, one losing—and it was with a great deal of uncertainty that we went into Election Day.

Astonishingly, we blew the opposition out, winning 56 percent to 44 percent. This was despite the fact that they'd spent $460,000 to our $30,000, which meant we'd been outspent about 15 to 1. It was not only a great victory for family-scale farmers but also a great victory for average people, who learned that they could, at least sometimes, defeat forces that seem so much more powerful. Initiative 300 is still in the Nebraska constitution 21 years later, in 2003, still protecting family farmers and ranchers, having survived challenges taken to the U.S. Supreme Court and repeated attacks from within the state.

And 14 years later, after my dad saw a *60 Minutes* segment on the horrific environmental damage suffered in North Carolina from factory hog farms, he called me to say how proud he was that I had helped protect

Nebraska from a similar fate. The circle was completed—it was one of the sweetest moments of my life.

MoveOn Tips

- Each state has its own rules and procedure for constitutional amendment; check your secretary of state's website to find out the relevant rules.

- For the complete text of the U.S. Constitution, go to www.usconstitution.net. This site also defines constitutional topics to help you better understand the electoral college and the amendment process.

- For the history of successfully ratified amendments, visit www.usconstitution.net/constamnotes.html.

- If you decide to try the initiative route, look at www.iandrinstitute.org, an excellent website for information on initiatives and referenda.

- Whatever route you choose, form a coalition with other like-minded groups—this spreads the workload and generates greater support. Call leaders of possible ally organizations, ask for a meeting, and use it to convince them to support your plan.

- Use free media to get your message out—make frequent use of press conferences, radio interviews, press releases, letters to the editor, and op-eds in newspapers. Also start your own website, and build an email list.

Alfred Dreyfus Samuelson has spent most of his adult life in progressive politics and is currently South Dakota Senator Tim Johnson's chief of staff. He's married and has two stepchildren.

Get a Socially Responsible Day Job

Julia Lamont, 25, Washington, DC

After graduating from college I decided to put my idealism to work and limit my job search to "socially responsible" organizations that were having a positive impact. Although many people, parents and peers alike, warned that I would be narrowing my options significantly, I knew that working for an organization I believed in would be the best motivation for me to excel in my career.

I ended up moving to Washington, DC, which was a great place for me because there is political information all around. Over time, my agitation about what was going on under the Bush Administration became more pronounced. I was not able to put it out of my mind, since so much of the action was happening in the city I lived in, down the street, in my backyard.

I applied for many jobs and went on informational interviews with people working in an array of fields. As I spoke with people, I became further convinced that working for an organization one likes and wants to be a part of has a huge effect on one's personal happiness.

After a few months of searching, I saw a job posting for EMILY's List, a Political Action Committee (PAC) that supports pro-choice Democratic women candidates early in their campaigns. As I read through the group's material, I became increasingly interested in the organization, because reproductive rights are one of the political issues I feel most strongly about.

I applied and got the job. I am extremely happy working at EMILY's List because it is actively doing something to change the direction of our country, and I know that my work here is a part of that process. Every day, I am surrounded by intelligent and motivated people who are all working toward a common goal. The best part of my experience was proving that I didn't have to "sell out" or "work for the man" in order to succeed in finding a job. My day job has meaning to me.

MoveOn Tips

- If you'd like to make your existing workplace more socially responsible, check the website of Businesses for Social Responsibility (www.bsr.org). It provides links and resources to support business decision making based on ethical values, respect for people, and respect for the community.

- Meiklejohn Civil Liberties Institute (www.mcli.org) publishes a *Human Rights Organizations and Periodicals Directory*, listing information about more than 1,200 progressive organizations and periodicals in the United States.

Julia Lamont graduated in 2001 with a B.A. in international relations and Russian studies. She now works at EMILY's List as the Major Gifts Coordinator.

Take Action with Your Family

Daud Azizi, 54, Lawrenceville, Georgia

I am a native of Afghanistan and a naturalized citizen of the United States. Having lived in Afghanistan, where I still have family, I sincerely appreciate the democratic process, civil liberties, and due process of law in the United States.

After the horror of 9/11, I wholeheartedly supported our troops going to Afghanistan to fight al Qaeda and liberate Afghanistan from the grip of the Taliban. However, when President Bush was preparing to attack Iraq, I became very concerned. In my mind, he had failed to show that we had the moral authority to attack Iraq. My concern grew as the opposition against the war grew both at home and abroad.

One day my daughter, Lena, came home crying because some high school classmates, while discussing Iraq, had commented, "We should kill them all." This was not an isolated incident. While sobbing, she asked me if there was any other place that we could go to get away from all of this. I was heartbroken, since I'd always considered that having my children born in the United States was absolutely the best thing I'd done for them. After feeling helpless for a few days, I decided that, for the love of my children and the love of this country, I could not sit still.

As a first step, I wrote a letter on the virtues of getting involved in the political process and voting. I distributed it to anyone who had an audience, including preachers, newspaper publishers, and radio talk show hosts. I started writing to my representative, John Linder, and my senators, urging them not to support the war on Iraq. I also regularly wrote to the Afghan Community Foundation to remind its members to register to vote.

As I followed MoveOn's Iraq antiwar campaign, I got interested in one presidential candidate in particular. My whole family then worked together to hold two fund-raising receptions in our house on behalf of the candidate. For one event I invited work colleagues and for the other, members of the Afghan Community Foundation. At each reception I gave a presentation on why the United States, which is the beacon of hope for the world, has to remain strong. I tried to emphasize that, if the neoconservatives surrounding the Bush Administration are not stopped, they will eventually bring this great nation down by making it an imperial power that lacks moral authority and that continually generates resentment by its preemptive strike policy.

Becoming involved in the political process at the grass roots has given my family hope for our future. We are very optimistic that this dark period in our history will not permanently damage us. I hope to leave no doubt in my children's minds that we live in the greatest country on earth, despite this temporary setback.

MoveOn Tips

- Pay attention to how your children and other family members are coping with political events.

- Involve your family in decisions to take action about issues that concern you.

- Listen to speeches or watch debates as a family, and afterward discuss what each family member thought about the event.

- Give your children a sense of their own power by having them participate with you in fund-raising, demonstrations, letter writing, or whatever activities you choose to express your political views.

Daud Azizi first came to the United States from Afghanistan in 1968 as an exchange student. He happily became a U.S. citizen in 1985, and he is now working with the Georgia Islamic Institute to get people to register to vote.

Host a Political Salon

Susan Oberman, 57, Charlottesville, Virginia

I have worked as part of the Charlottesville Center for Peace and Justice (CCPJ) since 1999. CCPJ began in 1983, and now, in addition to actions and outreach, our goals include nurturing and supporting one another by allowing for disagreements and individuality while working collaboratively. Paying attention to the importance of how we work together, in addition to our focus on tasks and goals, means that we strive to unite the personal and the political, recognizing and honoring our individual differences as resources that give us a broader view of what we are trying to accomplish. We use a dialogue process in committee meetings and at the CCPJ Salon. We are calling this a shared leadership model, using each person's unique gifts and encouraging us to teach these skills to one another.

The monthly salons are held in my home. We can accommodate 20 to 30 people. Each salon is planned by the committee and has a specific topic. Invitations and information on dialogue are sent to each person on the list for that month. The committee also researches websites and resources to provide literature on the topic, and those materials are available at the salon.

The evening begins with an icebreaker, usually some funny quotes or stories. This is followed by an introduction of the topic and of the dialogue process. Then we spend 45 minutes in small group dialogue on each person's experience with and feelings about the topic. Topics have included: "Trading Freedom for Security," "Oil and War," "The Politics of Food," and "Separation of Church and State."

For the second part of the evening, people choose a topic group in which to participate for about 45 minutes, discussing issues and possible actions. For the December 2003 topic on "Fabricated Wars: Greed Exposed," for example, the topic groups were:

1. How do we listen to discern truth from lies in the news?
2. How do we talk to other people about what we are seeing/feeling?
3. How do we deal with our fear and despair?

One of the committee members facilitates each group and offers information, tools, and ideas for action.

We end the formal part of the evening with feedback from the topic groups. People are then invited to stay, enjoy food and drink, and continue talking. These salons differ from some more traditional models because they aren't just about communication—there *is* a political agenda. Our discussions are directly connected to political action. The idea is that we need to talk to each other as much as we need to talk to the "powers that be" or those who disagree with us. And we need to come together to create change.

Dialogue is being used to deal with conflicts around the globe. By integrating it into our work we gain a sense of connection with all who are committed to peace and justice, all who believe these goals are not only possible but also of planetary urgency. The principles of dialogue that we use come from a variety of sources, primarily the Days of Dialogue program instituted by the Society for Professionals in Dispute Resolution and a coalition of groups that formed after the O. J. Simpson trial in Los Angeles. While the framework of the salon doesn't give us time to teach the dialogue process, we send materials in advance and attempt to practice dialogue at the salon, with gentle guidance by the committee members who serve as participant facilitators.

One of the sources of the concept of dialogue is Martin Buber, who said, "On the far side of the subjective, on this side of the objective, on the narrow ridge where I and Thou meet, there is the realm of the 'between'. . . . Here the genuine third alternative is indicated, the knowledge of which will help to bring about the genuine person again and to establish genuine community."

MoveOn Tips

- Follow the principles of dialogue:
  1. Listen with respect to all equally.
  2. Bring assumptions into the open.

3. Suspend judgment and reaction.

4. Speak for yourself truthfully; make "I" statements.

5. Expand the inquiry; ask questions.

Susan Oberman is a certified family mediator in Charlottesville, Virginia. She sees the "battle" in the family as a microcosm of the battles in the community, the nation, and the planet, which must be addressed on both the personal and the political level.

Let Your Money Speak

Anne Slepian, 47; Christopher Mogil, 47,
Arlington, Massachusetts

Imagine, if you can, that you are an idealistic 24-year-old, living and working as a community activist in a poor urban neighborhood. You answer the phone one day. A woman briskly announces that she's from a Wall Street investment firm and that the stock portfolio your grandmother willed to you is in the mail.

What is she saying? You don't even know what a portfolio is! You have been living near the poverty line. Few of your fellow activists—people you respect, many of whom are decades your senior—have even $1,000 in the bank. You are about to receive several hundred thousand times that amount. What do you do?

This was our life-changing experience in the early 1980s. It led us into a quest to discover how to use money to further our deepest values. When a second inheritance later came along (no longer taking us by surprise) we felt we already had enough, and so we committed it entirely to supporting social change. We also created a national nonprofit called More Than Money, to help others like ourselves use their financial resources to make a difference in the world. As a result of these actions, the meaning of money in our lives changed profoundly, from a recurrent source of anxiety to an energizing and influential tool.

So many of us who are out to "change the world" have negative beliefs and feelings about money. We view rich people as the bad guys of the planet. Money is evil to want; impossible to get. We never have enough, and, even if we did, we'd feel incompetent about managing it. If we are unusual in having more than we need, we often try to hide that fact, even from ourselves. All around us, there is a profound taboo against talking openly about our personal money situations. These beliefs (and many others) debilitate us and keep us from harnessing the full positive energy our money can have.

No matter what our resources are, our money can be a constructive force. Americans are living in the wealthiest country in the history of the planet. Instead of going to the mall or waiting for Bill Gates to fix things, we can take matters into our own hands and breathe life-giving power into the money we all have—which collectively is considerable.

MoveOn Tips

- Bank and invest your savings through institutions that work to strengthen local communities. Learn how at www.communityinvesting.org. You can even use your retirement funds to create change. Choose socially screened mutual funds (to combine growth with lower risk by being part of a big pooled fund); comparisons of these funds are given at www.communityinvesting.org and www.coopamerica.org. You can also invest in community development loan funds, microenterprise funds, and community development banks or credit unions, where your financial return is typically low but your money enables low-income people to build their livelihoods and buy their own homes (see www.communitycapital.org/community_development/).

- Spend at least a portion of your money on products and services that support fair wages and environmental sustainability. Check out www.coopamerica.org for listings of "green businesses" and more.

- Give proactively and more substantially to a few causes, organizations, or people that you believe are making a strategic difference. One place to view a variety of options and set up a giving fund is www.calvertfoundation.org.

- Plan how much you need long-term. An inexpensive financial software program (ideally, supplemented with advice from a financial planner) can help you do this. If you discover you have a financial surplus, decide how to give that money to create change. What could generate the biggest "bang for the buck" and be most thrilling to you personally?

> Check out www.morethanmoney.org to tap into a peer community exploring these questions.
>
> - Invite friends to join membership organizations such as www.newdream.org, to explore with you the difference our dollars can make. Collectively, we have amazing economic power.

Anne Slepian and *Christopher Mogil,* founders of More Than Money, are life partners who write, sing, organize, homeschool, direct a Playback Theatre company (www.truestorytheater.org), and consult about donor education (www.donorleaders.org).

Help Others Express Their Political Views

Caitlin Orr, 17, Fullerton, California

"Do We Really Want a Million New Terrorists?" I read every morning on an antiwar ad my mother had hung on our refrigerator door. "No way," my friends and I agreed, but we couldn't figure out how best to do our part to prevent the invasion of Iraq.

At last, it dawned on me: I could post these ads at school to get students involved with the peace movement. I posted at least 30 copies, and several of my teachers readily agreed to pin them up in their rooms. By the end of the day, though, all of the outside posters had either been torn down by the school administration or destroyed with phrases such as "Kill Saddam," and "Attack Iraq Now, I Want Cheaper Oil." I had to find a more permanent, unique, and involving way to protest.

What better way is there to get through to high school students than fashion? I reasoned. The Think Peace T-shirt was born. The shirt was black with a white peace sign on the front. It read: "Think Peace. Support the Anti-War Movement." The back of the shirt displayed my favorite bumper sticker slogan: "War doesn't decide who's right, only who's left." Within a week I had 58 orders from students and teachers eager to make a stand against the war. I asked people to wear the shirts every Friday.

The first Friday that students and teachers wore the shirts, the action was controversial. However, immediately, more orders came in. Friends said wearing the shirts made them feel they were at least doing *something*. I put in a second order. And then a third.

To the dismay of too many teachers, students, and administrators, my Think Peace shirts came out in full force every Friday. "Why are you so unpatriotic?" some of my classmates accused. "If I wasn't patriotic," I replied, "then why would I care what my country was doing?"

Two weeks later, I was interviewed by Daniel Yi, a reporter for the *Los Angeles Times*. I discussed the obstacles I'd faced—for example, my high school principal informed me that I couldn't sell the shirts on campus, and one offended teacher requested a permanent substitute on Fridays. After the interview, Yi told me he was impressed that a high school student could spark such a great debate. His article appeared on the front page of the "California" section of the *Times*.

Almost instantly letters and emails came in from admiring strangers. A friend helped me create a Think Peace website, and I ordered Think Peace business cards. I was interviewed by others in the media and contacted by amazing people. I was the youngest honoree of four at the yearly "Women Making a Difference in Orange County" awards ceremony, where I received commendations from our congresswoman and state senator. At peace rallies, I began to see my shirts worn by strangers. By my last count, over 700 people have bought a shirt, and I'm just getting ready to put in a new order.

People say I inspired them, but I just gave them a way to express the feelings they already had bottled up inside. When I started out, I felt like a nobody, but now I feel I've made a significant stand for something I feel passionate about. As Margaret Mead said, "Never doubt that a small group of thoughtful committed citizens can change the world." For me it all just started with "thinking peace."

MoveOn Tips

- Use the tools and resources of United for Peace (www.united-forpeace.org) to become active in the peace effort. Try links at that site to get your hands on the buttons, stickers, and signs you wish you had, to express your views.

Caitlin Orr is a senior at Fullerton High School, where she is founder and president of the P.E.A.C.E. club (People Ethically Against Conflict Everywhere). To find out more about Think Peace T-shirts, visit www.artandwebdesign.com/thinkpeace.

Express Your Views through Art

Kathryn Blume, 35, Charlotte, Vermont, and

New York, New York

I t was December 2002, and I was depressed. Being an out-of-work actor in New York is tough enough. Add to that an impending war on Iraq that you're sure will lead to Total Global Armageddon, and, well, that's the road to Utter Doom and Gloom. I tried writing letters, I tried attending rallies, I wrote apologetic letters to Arabic newspapers, I put a No War on Iraq sign in my window. But nothing felt like it had enough of an effect.

Finally, I heard about a new group in New York called THAW— Theatres Against War. It was planning a big day of action in March, and it encouraged theatre artists to produce something specifically for that day. I'd been working on a screenplay adaptation of Aristophanes' *Lysistrata*, an ancient Greek play in which war-weary women deny their men sex until the guys lay down their swords. It was too early in my writing process to show my adaptation, but I thought I could do a reading of the play, invite a few friends, and let that be my contribution.

I asked my friend Sharron Bower to work on the reading with me. She loved the idea. And then something happened. We started having one of those "Yes! And . . ." conversations, building upon each other's ideas. We decided to do it as a benefit for humanitarian aid in Iraq. We decided to cast a celebrity in the hope of raising more money. We thought maybe we could do more than one reading. Within 24 hours, we had decided to take it worldwide, and the Lysistrata Project was born.

We spent a few days building a website—a comprehensive online how-to kit for producing your own reading—and then we emailed everyone we knew, to announce the project. People thought it was a great idea and forwarded it to everyone they knew. Twice. People all over the country and around the world started volunteering to do readings.

By March 3, 2003, we'd had 1,029 readings in 59 countries and all 50 states. We were covered by major newspapers, magazines, radio programs, and TV news programs worldwide. People hosted readings at every level—in living rooms and teeny community theatres and major venues with really famous people, in trailer park diners and Kurdish refugee camps. There were secret readings in China and Jerusalem and another in northern Iraq—undertaken by members of an international press corps, who had to remain anonymous so they wouldn't get fired.

We didn't stop the war. But we know that providing a megaphone for voices of dissent was vitally important. Participants needed to know that their opinions mattered, to find a community of people who shared their opinions, and to make it clear to the world that George Bush wasn't speaking for all Americans. Everyone who wrote to us afterward said the same thing: that in the midst of tension and fear and frustration about not being heard by the press or the government, the reading was a raucous blessing.

MoveOn Tips

- Create a solid organizational structure, including a comprehensive website with press releases, talking points, and anything else that will make it easy for people to participate—no matter what the size of the event.

- Have defined goals that you can state clearly and succinctly, particularly when speaking to the press. Try not to deviate from the main message.

- Try to let go of all your expectations about the outcome. Ultimately, what results is completely outside of your control.

Kathryn Blume is an actor. Her latest project is touring a one-woman show called *The Accidental Activist,* describing her Lysistrata Project experience. For more information, go to www.LysistrataProject.com and www.TheAccidentalActivist.com.

Advertise Your Political Vision

Creighton Peet, 46, Pacific Grove, California

Like many Americans, I was as upset by our government's violent response to the attacks of September 11, 2001, as I was by the attacks themselves. By the fall of 2002, the Bush Administration was marching toward an unprecedented "preemptive" invasion of Iraq despite vocal, global condemnation. It would be hard to exaggerate my feelings of outrage, fear, and powerlessness.

I had been expressing my opposition by distributing posters at rallies, contributing to MoveOn, writing letters to the editor, and participating in peace vigils, but I needed to do more. I wanted to make a bigger impact in my own way.

On the lookout for opportunities, I became intrigued by the approaching 2003 Super Bowl weekend in San Diego. It seemed a unique chance to help legitimize and broaden a then-controversial peace message at a mainstream, all-American event. On a lark, I called an aerial advertising company one week before game day and discovered that there were still planes available.

Major advertisers had opted out because the coveted airspace over the stadium itself would be closed for security, but that didn't bother me—fans would be all over San Diego that weekend, and rates had dropped to a relative bargain: $375 an hour.

Beach towns like San Diego are perfect for aerial advertising, and numerous outdoor Super Bowl exhibitions and parties were scheduled, where captive audiences could easily see my plane. Another benefit of advertising this way was that I remained personally anonymous. I asked some friends to contribute, so the sponsors of the effort could be "a small group of private citizens."

MoveOn had just launched a national ad campaign with the tag line "Let the Inspections Work." I liked this pragmatic, hopeful appeal and believed it was about as radical a peace message as I could effectively put out at the Super Bowl. I wanted to help legitimize the peace movement for the American mainstream and perhaps nudge the public dialogue toward moderation and sanity.

MoveOn gave us its blessing, so I booked the plane and added an American flag to the banner to emphasize the patriotism behind our peaceful message. The weather in San Diego that weekend was beautiful, and people were outdoors everywhere. Our little plane flew over it all on both Saturday and Sunday for a grand total of four hours. We even circled the stadium before the game—reaching many corporate tailgaters, early arrivals, and gawkers.

I'll never know how many people actually saw our message. I know the potential audience, including secondary media coverage, was in the millions. For $1,500 I got a small piece of the same exposure and association with the Super Bowl as multi-million-dollar national advertisers.

With resourcefulness, creativity, and a small budget you can leverage big events and big crowds to get your message out in ways that have a disproportionately large impact. We dropped a pebble into the pond that weekend, having faith that its ripples would go where they were needed.

MoveOn Tips

- Any mass event can be a captive audience for your advertising. Make a list of major events and large venues in your community (concerts, festivals, sports activities, and the like).

- Check your local Yellow Pages under "Advertising." Look for aerial, outdoor, transit, or promotional advertising companies. Don't forget printers.

- Once you know the available opportunities and resources, think about a fun, personally meaningful way to speak out.

- Get inspired by examples of how others have used advertising resourcefully. In addition to MoveOn, check out www. CaliforniaPeaceAction.org, www.TomPaine.com, www. Fenton .com, www.Whitehouse.org, www.Micahwright.com, and www.CodePink4Peace.org.

- You don't need to use a plane: try mobile billboards, stationary billboards, newspaper and event program ads, flyers, posters, bumper stickers, and buttons. All of these make an impact.

Creighton Peet is a writer. He wants to remind readers that even the smallest effort toward honoring our genuine love of country makes a difference, especially when it feels most hopeless.

Afterword

Eli Pariser, Campaigns Director, MoveOn

Here's my story: On September 11, 2001, I was 20 years old.

When the planes struck the World Trade Center, and the Pentagon, and the ground in Pennsylvania, I reacted in the same way that the rest of America did. I was horrified.

The next day, as the president and the politicians began their public statements, my thoughts turned to the future. I was concerned that a response to the attacks based on vengeance would bring with it even greater tragedies in the years ahead. That evening, I created a small website—a site that laid out some constructive, multilateral ideas for the American response to the attacks. I included a petition to President Bush and other world leaders. Late that night, I sent out a message about it to 30 friends.

One morning about a week later, I woke up to find thousands of messages from strangers in my email inbox. Then the server started to crash; there were too many people trying to access my site. By the end of that week, my little website was one of the top 500 on the Internet. I got a call from a Romanian journalist who had received the petition by email five different times from five different people. It traveled by word of mouth. People sent the email on to their friends and families, who in turn sent it to their friends and families.

Two weeks later, over 500,000 people from 192 countries had signed the petition. They wanted to write letters, so I helped them write letters. They wanted to make phone calls, so I provided the numbers. I began to work with MoveOn.org and together we organized hundreds of congressional visits, delivered petitions representing hundreds of thousands of people to Congress, and raised millions for ads that countered the Bush Administration's spin. We grew from a few hundred thousand to over 2.3 million members. On February 15, 2003, we contributed to the largest day of protest in the history of the world.

But when I started the website on my laptop in my living room, I couldn't have imagined any of this was about to unfold. I didn't have any grandiose thoughts of a global movement. I didn't even know if my web-site would resonate among my friends. I just was contributing what I could at a time when I felt the country demanded it of me.

Looking back, I'm reminded that we never quite know what's going on at the time. We don't know whether a story is beginning or ending, or what part we're playing. Often, we don't know what the story is really about.

A few days ago, Joan Blades and I were talking about reading the newspaper. Joan said, "I have to admit, I never used to follow current events. My assumption was that a year from now, whatever was taking up pages and pages today could be summarized in a paragraph or two, and you could save a lot of reading."

It's not a bad point. The events that consume us now will resolve themselves over time—receding from the front pages of newspapers into books, from books into chapters, from chapters into paragraphs, and from paragraphs into footnotes. If you have the patience, it makes a kind of sense to wait for the CliffsNotes version.

But there's a big problem with being this kind of reader. The problem with waiting for the national story to unfold is that we're all characters in it. And by the time we begin to understand it, our opportunity to change how the story ends will be gone.

Most of the stories in this book were submitted in response to one MoveOn email in September 2003. They represent a fraction of the stories that came in, which were themselves a tiny fraction of the stories that are out there. The personal accounts in this book are a drop in the ocean.

Some of these stories are just the prologues to much bigger tales— how bad corporate initiatives will be defeated, or how good people will be elected, or how the United States will regain the respect of the world. And some of them will end right here, barely remembered a few years from now. The thing is, we don't know which.

That's why this book isn't just about the individual stories. The common thread that weaves them together is the story of democracy, a story that is still unfinished. We don't know yet whether it will end in tragedy or in joy or somewhere in between. The only way to find out how it ends is to keep writing it.

Get out a pen.

Start the next chapter.

Acknowledgments

We want to thank MoveOn members for their efforts on behalf of our country. People are starting to look at grassroots support in a whole new, infinitely more respectful way. In particular, we want to thank each and every MoveOn member who wrote a story for this book. We received over 2,500 wonderful stories. We kept asking, "Can't we make it 100 ways to love your country?" because it was so hard to not share all the stories. Thank you for your exuberant support.

It took a great collective effort—and democratic process!—to produce this book. First, we want to thank Karen Bouris, associate publisher at Inner Ocean Publishing, for her persistence in encouraging MoveOn to publish a book. She believed we could engage an even broader audience in the political dialogue through a powerful, inspiring book—and we hope we have succeeded. We didn't know if we could take on one more project, but Karen convinced us and helped us figure out how to make it possible. And she found a talented editor, Angela Watrous, who has been amazing in working with the many contributors and doing the lion's share of the work necessary to create a book like this. There were many behind-the-scenes people, from copy editors to designers, publicity mavens to dedicated salespeople, whose passion and commitment to the book have been overwhelming. Remarkably, most of these people have been MoveOn members from the beginning.

Then there is the MoveOn team. Each of them is incredibly talented and committed. We are honored to be working with these people.

Index

MoveOn Information

The MoveOn family of organizations consists of three entities. MoveOn.org, a 501(c)(4) organization, primarily focuses on education and advocacy on important national issues. MoveOn.org PAC, a federal PAC, primarily helps members elect candidates who reflect our values. And MoveOn.org Voter Fund, a 527 organization, primarily runs ads exposing President Bush's failed policies in key "battleground" states.

These sites can be found at:

www.MoveOn.org

www.MoveOnPAC.org

www.MoveOnVoterFund.org

For information about MoveOn's Media Corps, go to www. moveon .org / mediacorps/.

For more information about contributions to any of our organizations, contact us at info@moveon.org or go to www.MoveOn.org and click on "Make a Donation."